TONQUIN BY THE SAVAGES OF THE N.W. COAST

ETAILED DRAWING OF THE SHIP *TONQUIN*

VOYAGES TO THE SOUTH SEAS, INDIAN AND PACIFIC OCEANS, CHINA SEA, NORTHWEST COAST, FEEJEE ISLANDS, SOUTH SHETLANDS, &c., &c.

VOYAGES

TO THE

SOUTH SEAS, INDI

NORTHWEST COAS

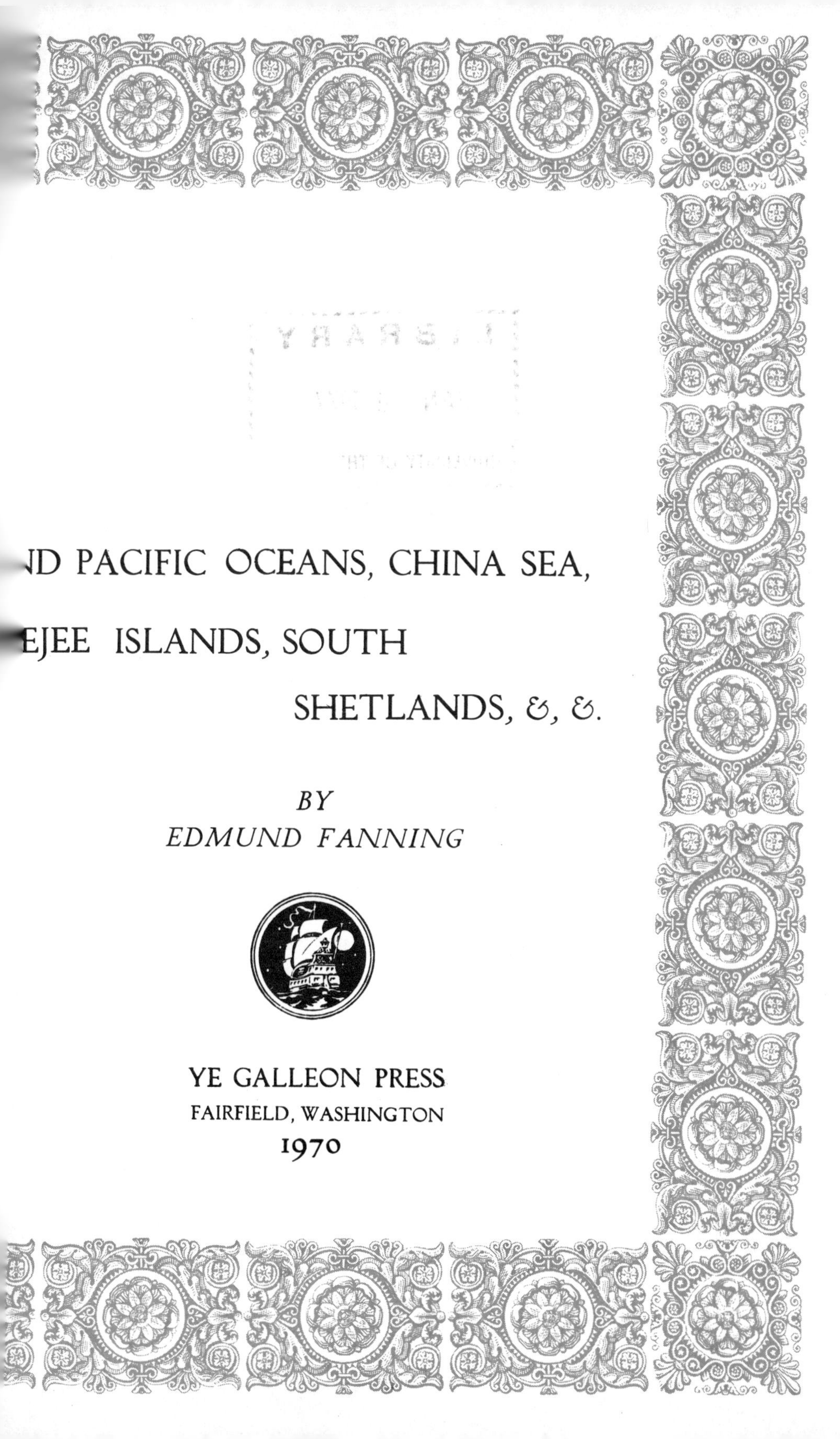

ND PACIFIC OCEANS, CHINA SEA,
EJEE ISLANDS, SOUTH
SHETLANDS, &, &.

BY
EDMUND FANNING

YE GALLEON PRESS
FAIRFIELD, WASHINGTON
1970

This work is not listed in Smith's Pacific Northwest but is listed as F-28 in Wright Howes' US-IANA.

Of this book 600 *Copies were printed.*

This is Copy Number 130 .

RAMSEY.

RAMSAY (Lamazee), sole survivor of the Tonquin massacre, was interpreter and guide on the fatal voyage. He is shown here sketched by Lt. Charles Wilkes in 1841. According to Rev. J. H. Frost, George Ramsay lost one eye before 1834 when it was scratched out by a hair seal.

Capt. Edmund Fanning House, Stonington, Conn. 1902

FANNING ARMS

INTRODUCTION

Edmund Fanning was a sea captain and merchant in the early American China fur trade. He was also a statesman and man of vision. Too little has been written of him.

A Connecticut-born Yankee, his cruises into the South Pacific and Atlantic oceans commencing in the 1790's yielded significant gains to American enterprise and discovery. He conceived and promoted in the nation's capital a plan to explore the south seas but he was too old by the time the Charles Wilkes expedition finally sailed in 1838; his name hardly appears in this respect.

Today we read of his achievements only in connection with the last voyage of the *Tonquin;* this was an expedition to the northwest coast which ended in the massacre of the entire ship's crew off Vancouver Island in 1811. This was an historic incident and Fanning presents in this volume an original version of the event. The ship had been built in 1807 at his direction, and he regarded it as a superior and first rate vessel. Fanning was the first commander of the *Tonquin* and after its second voyage to the south seas for sandalwood he sold it to John Jacob Astor. The ship was under Astor's company when it was attacked and destroyed. Fanning obviously had a strong attachment to this vessel but it played just a part in his total operations, of some seventy voyages, on the seas of the world.

The choice, therefore, to republish this book, Fanning's second and completely different volume, was not a difficult one to make. First, Edmund Fanning was a prime promoter of American interests in the South Pacific. He was one of our nation's first sea captains to sail around the world with an all American crew. Secondly, his first book (1833) on his early south sea voyages was brought out again in 1924 by the Marine Research Society and this is still available in the rare book market. However, his 1838 volume has never been republished. Thirdly, these voyages of adventure and discovery in the Pacific and other seas stir the imagination and give cause to wonder at the courage and fortitude of the sailors who sought out, in their small wooden ships, the uncharted ports and strange peoples of an earlier era.

This book was published under the following title:

Voyages to the South Seas, Indian and Pacific Oceans, China Sea, North-West Coast, Feejee Islands, South Shetlands, &c. &c. with an account of the new discoveries made in the southern hemisphere, between the years 1830-1837 . . . By Edmund Fanning. Second Edition. New York: *William H. Vermilye.* 1838. 324 p., front., 19 cm.

By comparison, his first book published in 1833 contained entirely different subject matter. This included his first voyage around the world as captain of the *Betsey* from 1797 to 1799; his cruises on the *Aspasia, Volunteer* and *Sea Fox* to the southern oceans for fur seal skins; and his agency directed voyages of the *Catharine, Union* and the *Seraph* and *Annawan* expedition. Except in isolated references, these vessels were not mentioned in his later work. The 1833 volume was published as:

Voyages Round the World; with selected sketches of Voyages to the South Seas, North and South Pacific Oceans, China, etc., performed under the command and agency of the author. Also, information relating to important Late Discoveries; between the years 1792 and 1832, together with the report of the commander of the first American exploring expedition, patronised by the United States government, in the brigs Seraph and Annawan, to the southern hemisphere. By Edmund Fanning. New York: *Collins* & *Hannay*. 1833. 499p., front., 23 cm.

In this first work (Chapter XXIV), the captain gave an indication of plans for a second volume:

"It is as well perhaps here to state, for the better understanding of the reader, that the details of the preceding chapters, and recorded in this volume, form but a very limited portion of the many voyages made by, or under the agency of the author; these in all amount to upwards of seventy, and furnish matter sufficient for a second volume; in fact, some difficulty has been experienced in making the selections which compose this volume, from the mass. Among the remainder are some accounts, with the particulars of which in all probability there are some few who may still have them in remembrance; such as the voyage of the ship Tonquin to China, and the many singular occurrences during the same, with the final destruction of that excellent ship, after a hard fought battle, with the hordes of savages on the north-west coast, who had gained possession of her deck, and forced the gallant Thorn, of the United States' navy, mortally wounded, to his cabin, where finding farther opposition fruitless, he applied the match to her magazine, thus in one instant hurling death upon his savage enemies who then thronged the decks.

"The voyage of the brig Hersilia, Captain J. P. Sheffield, and an account of her capture at Arauco, on the coast of Chili, by that noted piratical general, or chief. Beunevidas, together with the aid and handsome treatment received on the occasion, from that gallant British naval officer, Commodore T. M. Hardy, then in command of the British force in the Pacific; as also the narrative of a young New Zealand chief, who, in compliance with the desire of his father, was brought to this country in the ship Hope, Captain O. Chase; he resided in the author's family upwards of twelve months, and is now reported to be in his father's former place, at the head of a powerful tribe."

As Fanning wrote above in his 1833 book, the second volume did contain the voyages of the *Tonquin, Hersilia* and also of the *Hope.* As a matter of fact, this volume, which you are about to read, includes the only known record today of the first two cruises of the *Tonquin.* (This "superior . . . gallant ship" made two New York to Canton trading runs between 1807 and 1809, before its fatal voyage of 1810.)

Brief comment should be made of the various printings of Fanning's books. Joseph Sabin's *Dictionary of Books relating to America* list a London (1834) and a French version as following the 1833 volume. His new book of 1838, republished herewith, was followed by three separate printings; the original however was listed as *Second Edition* (and Sabin cites thereafter the Fourth Edition and Fifth Edition, and the writer was able to locate the Third Edition under the U.S. Library of Congress Catalog of Printed Cards.) Needless to say, any of these printings of the two volumes must now be classified as exceedingly rare books.

Mention should also be made of the 1924 reprint of Fanning's first book. This was published as:

Voyages & Discoveries in the South Seas, 1792-1832 By Captain Edmund Fanning, A Native of Stonington, Conn. Salem, Massachusetts: Marine Research Society. 1924. 335 p., front., plates. 24½ cm.

Though this title is different, the contents are the same as the 1833 volume. The notable exception is that it omits Chapters XXIII, XXIV and XXV which are the last three chapters of the original. Some mention of the contents should be made because these are now the only parts of Fanning's books which have not been republished.

Chapter XXIII is headed: "Recommendations, founded on experience, for doubling Cape Horn for the Pacific, with some views upon the practicability of advancing and penetrating to the South Pole." Fanning here suggests that ships, facing gales from the west, should avoid the "ancient and long followed course between Cape Horn and the South Shetland Islands, either of the two following routes being . . . preferable." He advises single vessels to keep close to the cape, three leagues or less, affording shelter from the westerlies. For fleets or squadrons, he recommends that the southbound course be maintained boldly until the South Shetlands are sighted. Between 62° and 65° degrees south latitude the ships will meet "with a fair south-east wind, which will enable her quickly to run up her western course." Regarding a penetration to the South Pole, Fanning drew from Captain James Weddell the plan to sail south on a course east of Palmer Peninsula. He urged an expedition for "reaching the South Pole, or making new discovery of land, which perhaps in value may far exceed our imagination . . ."

In Chapter XXIV, Fanning related his attempt (1829-30) to sail to the South Pole or the Antarctic continent, whichever would be reached first. As agent, he sent Captains Benjamin Pendleton and Nathaniel Palmer on the brigs *Seraph* and *Annawan* to the icy seas off Cape Horn. Captain Palmer had already distinguished himself by co-discovering the South Orkney Islands and then exploring Palmer Archipelago in 1821. Searching for lands to the southwest, they encountered rough seas and cold, rugged weather. With "our crews . . . worn down by fatigue, and from their being almost constantly wet in this region . . . with at the same time alarming symptoms of that dread disease the scurvy making its appearance; it was considered most advisable to bear up and proceed for the coast of Chili, there to refresh and recruit our men as well as to replenish our wood and water." Thus ended another of Fanning's expeditions with little or no credits, by way of discovery, to himself.

Chapter XXV, the last in Fanning's first book, reveals the commission he received from President Madison in 1812 to lead a discovery expedition "of the southern hemisphere, and voyage round the world." Before the ships could sail, war was declared by the Congress against Great Britain and the expedition was suspended. (This proved to be but a preview of his fortunes in seeking national eminence.)

Aboard ship, Fanning was a wise and careful navigator. He apparently had the full loyalties of his crews.

His first voyage around the world was as commander of the brig *Betsey* in which he had only a one-eighth share. A small vessel, it was "a little short of 100 tons." But this size proved a blessing, for she was able to safely clear a number of submerged coral reefs in the Pacific which larger vessels may have struck.

It is well to relate a few of Fanning's adventures from his first book, covering his first voyages, as background to this second volume. The voyage on the *Betsey* was a milestone in developing trade across the far-flung Pacific islands.

With this cruise he also made the one discovery of lasting notice. On June 11, 1798, he discovered three uninhabited islands while sailing west about 1,000 miles south of Hawaii. To these were given the name "Fanning's Islands." The next day his crew sighted another, which the Captain named Washington Island. These are now called the Line Islands, and Fanning Island has a relay station on the transpacific cable.

Leaving these islands, the *Betsey* sailed ever westward towards Canton, carrying in her holds a full cargo of fur seal skins. On June 14th, Fanning wrote "we had the weather quite pleasant, with a brisk trade breeze, nor has there been any necessity, while sailing over or across the western part of this extensive Pacific ocean, to lay the ship by a single night, through fear of running her upon any hidden danger . . ."

The crew was confident enough to sail through each night; but these were uncharted waters, and was this confidence justified?

That night at nine Captain Fanning retired to his berth as customary. An hour later he awoke and found himself on the upper steps of the companion way. He exchanged a few words with the officer on watch and returned to his cabin, thinking that he had never before walked in his sleep. Twenty minutes later he again came to himself in the same location and answered to the officer's question that he felt quite all right. Wondering what had brought him twice to the companion way he inquired as to visibility about the ship. He was assured that over one mile of ocean could be seen, and with a strange sensation upon his mind he retired to his berth.

For the third time he was astonished to find himself on the steps, and this time, without being aware of it, he had put on his clothes and hat. He then conceived some danger close by, and the vessel was running the seas under full sail at five knots. He ordered the sails taken in and the ship brought to. The station was to be maintained until daylight when he would be called. It was necessary for the captain to reassure the officer that he did possess his full senses. With this done, he enjoyed a sound sleep until called at dawn.

A favorable report brought the order to make all sail, and after some minor duties below, Fanning came on deck just as the first rays of the sun splashed over the clear eastern horizon. The crew were all busily engaged and he walked the quarter deck. On taking a brief glance forward, the "whole truth flashed" before his eyes. There were breakers, mast high, dirctly ahead and towards which the ship was fast sailing.

Instantly he placed the helm a lee and the sails trimmed by the wind as the man aloft called out, "breakers, breakers ahead!"

No one spoke except for the needed orders given. The roar of the herculean breakers was clearly heard from a short mile away. The officer of the night watch came up to the captain.

"Why, Sir," he said, "half an hour's farther run from where we lay by in the night, would have cast us on that fatal spot, where we must all certainly have been lost. If we have, because of the morning haze around the horizon, got so near this appalling danger in broad daylight, what, Sir, but the hand of Providence, has kept us clear of it through the night."

Fanning was convinced that "this premonition, so unusual . . . (was) as an evidence of the Divine superintendence, and there, ever will remain so firmly imprinted . . ." The *Betsey* had weathered off to the north, and the crew had a fair view of the coral reef in the form of a crescent, six leagues in length; and within the crescent was white shoal water. Had the ship run upon it at night, he was certain, all should have perished.

In October 1798 a profitable trade for China goods was made at Canton. On the thirtieth they passed Macao on the first leg to New York via the Indian ocean. Another vessel from Philadelphia had joined them. On passing through the strait between Sumatra and Java, a bay on the Sumatra side opened up to them. Suddenly a fleet of proas, the swift Malaysian vessels usually manned by pirates, burst from the bay.

The pirate fleet, numbering twenty-nine, put on a "bold and defying front." To the surprise of the *Betsey's* crew, the Philadelphia ship "so soon as she had the pirates in view, hauled on a wind for the Java shore, and being a far superior sailer . . . soon left her, disregarding our signals for them to stand by . . ."

The enemy ships, assured by the flight of the larger consort, "gave chase after us, in three divisions, making use of all their sails and oars . . . never ceasing as they came on, to pass signals of some kind from one division to another."

On the American ship, "all hands were at quarters, and with our eight four-pounders of iron, and two brass long six-pound guns, each charged with a round shot and bag of musket balls, we waited the approach of these marauders." Captain Fanning asked each man to be firm in his duty and expressed confidence in their actions.

One of the pirate divisions pushed forward directly under the *Betsey's* stern, "while within a quarter of a mile on each side were the other two divisions, seemingly advancing with the intention of falling on our bows . . ." The captain directed his attention to their signals, for their leader or admiral appeared to be in the right wing and this was the division likely to begin the action.

The attackers opened musket fire and began shouting at the same time. Their savage appearance would have been creditable to a party of wild Indians.

At this moment Fanning made his move. "I clapped the helm a weather, hauled up the courses, and the ship, quickly wearing off, brought her broadside as handsomely as mortal could wish, to bear directly on the proas.

"We let them have it, in this the first discharge dismasting the centre vessel, and disabling two on each side of her; the effect produced was as expected; they instantly stopped their headway by means of their sweeps, and were apparently making up their minds as to, how next, we now wore ship again, and the better to assist their meditations, gave them another broadside with a suitable proportion of musketry.

"Their admiral then concluded to make the signal for a retreat, which was very promptly obeyed by the whole body moving off with the disabled proas . . .

"By the time we had again made sail on our course, the piratical fleet were quite out of sight, having entered a river or creek up the bay . . . while far away in the southwest quarter, not to be seen from the deck, and only faintly discernable from the mast-head, was our valiant consort."

The *Betsey,* after a passage of 178 days from Canton, arrived at New York on April 26, 1799. The cargo of China, teas and silks was sold; even when the investment in the ship and all overhead costs were deducted, there still remained a net profit of $52,300. The duties paid into the nation's treasury, alone, were three times the original investment.

"Thus successfully terminated the author's first voyage around the world . . . without the loss of a man." Fanning believed this to be the first American vessel wholly manned by native citizens ever to sail around the globe from the port of New York.

BIOGRAPHICAL

Only one source of information on Edmund Fanning is known, other than his own two books. This is the short biography by Walter Frederic Brooks, *History of the Fanning Family,* two vols., Worcester, Massachusetts, printed privately, 1905.

A few other references can be found. Don C. Seitz in his book *Uncommon Americans,* Indianapolis, Bobbs-Merrill Co., 1925, devotes ten pages to Fanning. This amounts to a review of his second book with emphasis on the *Tonquin* voyages. In the monumental work by P. C. Phillips and J. W. Smurr, *The Fur Trade,* two vols., Norman, University of Oklahoma Press, 1961, Captain Fanning is given one-half of a page.

The most recent biographical sketch of him appears in *Five Sea Captains,* edited by Walter Teller, New York, Atheneum Publ., 1960. This book extracts from Fanning's 1833 edition his complete account of the voyage of the *Betsey,* 1797-99. Mr. Teller also includes a very well written, brief biography, using primarily the Brooks source.

Edmund Fanning was born in Stonington, Connecticut, on July 16, 1769. He was the sixth son of a large family of eleven children. His parents, Gilbert and Huldah (Palmer) Fanning chose the side of the colonists in the Revolutionary War.

One of his uncles was General Edmund Fanning, an Englishman, and this relationship was of considerable help to the younger Edmund in later years. At least twice, the younger Fanning was able to avert the impounding of his ships and impressment of his crews by the British, by the strength of this kinship. The captain was first and foremost a sea merchant and there is no reference in his two books of any ill feeling towards the British.

He took to the sea at the age of fourteen, beginning as cabin boy. Embracing a seafaring life, he rose through the regular grades of seaman, second mate, first mate and captain. Following return of the *Betsey* to New York in 1799, he attained recognition as one of the most successful navigators of that century. That voyage opened up new avenues of Pacific trade.

Fanning next took command of the corvette *Aspasia* in January 1800. At the South Georgia Islands, east of Cape Horn in the South Atlantic, he acquired 57,000 fur seal skins. He then sailed to Canton to exchange the skins for China goods. Charting his course around the Cape of Good Hope for his second voyage around the world, he arrived at New York on March 4, 1802.

In both of his books, he explained in detail the prolific animal life of the Falklands and other southern islands. They abounded in seals, sea lions and sea elephants, wild hogs and pigs, geese, ducks, albatross and penguins. In later voyages when the seal rookeries were depleted, his ships carried to Canton cargoes of sandalwood, mother-of-pearl and even the marine worm highly prized by the grocers of China. The sandalwood was a fragrant wood from various trees used for chests, fans and ornamental work. Distilling the wood in chips yielded an oily perfume. The sandalwood islands were found in the most western part of the Pacific.

During his many voyages he developed the idea for a United States sponsored expedition to the south seas. The purpose was to be "for national benefit to navigation, commercial trade, the whale and seal fisheries, science, &c." He petitioned Congress several times, beginning in 1831, for a National Discovery and Exploring Expedition to the South Seas.

The Congress finally authorized the expedition in May 1836 but the measure was included in the Navy's appropriation bill. This meant that civilian leadership was excluded. The expedition was thereafter plagued with bureaucratic difficulties. Fanning, by mail, protested the plan to use too many and too large ships, unsuitable for sailing the unchartered coral islands.

As evident in the book, following, Fanning devoted the Appendix to the plans for the expedition. Excluded from it, he asked only for "justice to be given on the volume of the records of the voyage . . . to the author . . ." The fleet was finally placed under Lieutenant Charles Wilkes and sailed from Norfolk in August 1838.

Until his death on April 23, 1841, at the age of 72, he was petitioning Congress for a proper exploring expedition to the high latitudes. Wilkes returned in 1842, having charted a large portion of the Pacific and the Antarctic. He had also explored the west coast of America in 1841. Nineteen volumes of the official report were thereafter printed. Fanning's name cannot be located among them.

NOTES ON THE VOYAGE OF THE "HOPE"

Part I of this book tells of the cruise of the *Hope,* 1806-08, and its adventures among the Fijis and other south sea islands.

Though Fanning writes in the first person, he was not on board. The *Hope* left New York on August 31, 1806, yet Fanning himself was to take over the newly built *Tonquin* which sailed on May 26, 1807. The first voyage of this new vessel was swift indeed, for she returned to New York on March 6, 1808, two months ahead of the *Hope*.

Edmund Fanning, in using the first person, spoke for the *Hope's* captain, Reuben Brumley, who was employed under the former's agency. In writing of this voyage, Fanning undoubtedly used Brumley's logbook which now can be found at Harvard University. (Reuben Brumley, "Log of the ship *Hope,*" 1806-08, MS in Baker Library, Harvard.)

As can be read, the voyage from New York around South Africa to the Fijis for sandalwood, then to Canton for teas and China goods, was very profitable for the Fanning agency. (The ship returned to New York again by way of the Cape of Good Hope.)

In addition to procuring his own cargo, Brumley paid and contracted for, with King Tynahoa, a load of sandalwood for the *Tonquin.* (This was picked up in December 1808 by this latter vessel, Captain Brumley also in command, being the second voyage of the famous ship.)

The *Hope's* crew, late in 1806, on the long run down the entire length of the Atlantic, came down with scurvy. The first adequate supply of fruits and vegetables was obtained at Port Jackson (Sydney, Australia). Leaving there, she sailed into the South Fiji Basin, lush with birds, an abundance of fish, countless coral islands and coconut and breadfruit crops and "large swarms of natives" many of whom were cannibals.

At Tongatapu, Captain Brumley made every attempt to learn of survivors of the ill-fated *Union,* Captain Isaac Pendleton. This vessel (as Fanning explains in his 1833 book, Chapter XVI) was under his agency in 1804 to obtain fur seal skins in the South Indian ocean. Having warehoused 14,000 skins, Pendleton sailed for Tongatapu where he and several crewmen were massacred while on shore for trading. The *Union* escaped only temporarily. Some months later under Captain Wright she returned to the Fiji for sandalwood and was driven upon a coral reef.

Wrote Fanning: "Every person on board either perished by drowning, or was massacred by the natives, who . . . had been watching every movement, and as each unfortunate man gained a foothold on the rocks, thus terminated his existence; their bodies, as has been subsequently ascertained, serving the purpose of food, for it will be remembered that these islanders are cannibals."

The *Hope* was the next vessel out under Fanning's agency and bore his specific instructions to search for survivors. But, as he observed on page 64 in the book following, Captain Brumley found none. He could only name the place of the wreck as Union Passage.

During the summer of 1807 the ship's crew procured a cargo of sandalwood from Toconroba, Fiji (the first such cargo by Americans from this group.) In addition, the contract with King Tynahoa for a second cargo was very specific. The wood was to be cut and piled up on a small island within eighteen months, there to await another ship of the owners. Beating out the competition, as it turned out, in the active spirit of the Pacific trade, Captain Brumley and his first officer, Mr. Brown, had managed this exclusive treaty by a unique gift: they constructed for the King a fourteen foot treasure chest, complete with gaudy colors, compartments with padlocks (and lengthy instructions on their use) and filled with the choice trade goods from the ship. Such diplomacy had its rewards, for fifteen months later, on December 11, 1808, Brumley returned on the *Tonquin* and found "our treaty cargo of sandalwood cut, shaved, and piled . . . already in waiting for us." Fanning was also impressed "with what good faith this royal monarch, over an uncivilized mass of beings . . . kept this treaty."

NOTES ON THE VOYAGES OF THE TONQUIN

As Fanning here presents in Part III, this was a "beautifully modelled and first-rate ship" and she was built with a copper bottom, double-flushed deck. "Pierced for 22 guns," she "proved a fast sailing vessel, of speed, perhaps, equal to any sloop of war of the navy."

The writer has wondered as to the origin of this name, and the answer seems to be found in the Encyclopedia Americana.

This defines "Tonquin, variant of Tonkin (q. v.)"

"Tonkin or Tongking, former name of the northern part of Vietnam, the region called Bac Bo by the Vietnamese. The name Tonkin (in French first called Tonquin) was given to the Vietnamese north by European explorers and missionaries of the sixteenth century."

The drawing of the attack and massacre of the crew of the *Tonquin* was the frontispiece of Fanning's original 1838 volume, and it is republished herewith. The reader will note that it shows eleven gun ports on the starboard side, thus substantiating his narrative as being "pierced for 22 guns."

The vessel was built under his "superintendence and inspection" by Adam and Noah Brown in New York. It should be assumed, therefore, that the drawing is quite accurate as to detail.

As noted earlier, the *Tonquin's* first voyage was under Captain Fanning and lasted just over nine months in

1807-08. Her outward cargo was not stated but was apparently loaded in New York as she sailed directly for Canton (via the Cape of Good Hope.)

On November 18, 1807, a unique meeting occurred in the harbor below Canton. The *Tonquin* met the ship *Hope,* Captain Brumley, "belonging to the same owners, Messrs. E. and H. Fanning, and W. Coles, merchants in the city of New York." Some 12,000 miles from his home port, Fanning exchanged a friendly visit with the captain of another ship of his small firm.

As may be read, Fanning next was blockaded in the harbor by British men-of-war, along with ten other American vessels. It was the *Tonquin* which volunteered to run the British line. Though fired upon and subsequently boarded, Fanning used his skill at diplomacy. He surrendered his ship, an intentional embarrassment of the English since no war then existed. One day later the British commander ordered all of the American ships released, and a possible earlier war was avoided. The *Tonquin* returned safely on the same route.

Though an embargo of United States ports was in effect, Fanning applied for another voyage in 1808. The argument presented to the nation's capitol was that the sandalwood was cut and ready in the Fijis and that considerable gains were due the U.S. treasury. The *Tonquin* was permitted to sail from New York on June 15th under Captain Brumley. Skirting the south coast of Australia, she traded the sandalwood at Canton and returned to her home port towards the close of 1809.

In 1810, the vessel was purchased by John Jacob Astor. Her fate on this third voyage is well known and Fanning's account, beginning on page 137, was given him by Captain James Sheffield of the *Hersilia.* He, in turn, had on board in 1823-24 the interpreter Lamayzie who was also the sole survivor of the *Tonquin* massacre. The story of the native interpreter has raised many questions over the past century, particularly as to the location of the disaster off Vancouver Island.

On September 6, 1810, the Astor vessel, under Captain Jonathan Thorn, sailed from New York on her last voyage. On board was a crew of twenty-one, plus thirty-three passengers. These latter were in the employ of the Pacific Fur Company and were the officers, clerks, boatmen and mechanics.

The *Tonquin's* last cargo consisted of goods imported the previous fall from London: drygoods, hardware, molasses, brandy and gin, plus four and one-half tons of gunpowder apparently intended for the Russian post at New Archangel.

After anchoring in the mouth of the Columbia river, from where some supplies were transferred to the new trading post at Astoria, Thorn again made sail. The *Tonquin* departed on June 5, 1811, and was never seen again by white men.

Fanning's account of the Indian attack off Vancouver Island differs from other accounts (Franchere, Ross, Cox). An analysis of these differences, plus a list of references to the vessel's last voyage, was presented by F. W. Howay in "The Loss of the Tonquin," *Washington Historical Quarterly,* Vol. XIII, No. 2 (April, 1922), 83-92.

In the past few decades, there have been many expeditions to search for the remains of the *Tonquin*. This vessel, after all, is famous for its part in creating the first permanent American settlement on the northwest coast. One article telling of such expeditions is "To Vancouver Island After the Tonquin," by this writer, *Canadian Geographical Journal*, Vol. LXI, No. 6 (December, 1960), 212-217.

These searches are now concentrated in Clayoquot Sound, although the Nootka Indians were known to have taken the *Boston* in 1803; this occurred to the north of Clayoquot, and another account (i.e. by Peter Corney, *Early Voyages in the North Pacific* 1813-1818, Fairfield, Washington, Ye Galleon Press, 1965) places the last location of the *Tonquin* off Checleset Bay. George M. Dawson, the Canadian, in 1887 gave the location as being at Cape Sutil, Nahwitti Bar.

George Davidson, the noted geographer, conducted an extensive search for the *Tonquin* from 1890 to 1896. One of his principals was John Devereux whose letters on this subject were recently located among the Davidson manuscript collection, Bancroft Library.

NOTES ON THE LOCATION OF "TONQUIN ISLAND" IN THE PACIFIC

On the *Tonquin's* second voyage from New York, Captain Reuben Brumley departed with a full load of sandalwood from Fiji, destined for Canton. On April 5, 1809, the lookout aloft cried "land, ho! which proved to be an extensive island, or islands . . . Being a new discovery, I gave the name Tonquin Islands . . . The centre . . . had the appearance of a ship water passage between the Islands, or lands, and a small rocky Islet lay at a short distance to the northward . . . we place in latitude 11°52′ south, and longitude 169°44′ east of London . . ."

The search for Tonquin Island on modern charts seems futile. The available maps of Melanesia do not reveal this island nor do the gazetteers or U.S. Hydrographic Office charts list such a place. The nearest land to these coordinates is Anuda (formerly, Cherry) Island (11°35′S., 169°51′E.) which is only one and one-half miles in length; Hydrographic Office Publication No. 81 indicates that it has a rock offshore from the north side. Possibly the best choice of "Fanning's discovery" would be Fataka (Mitre) Island, 26 miles southeast of Anuda. Fataka, when seen from the east, appears as two separate haycocks; these are two hills approximately 400 feet high. There is also a high rock on the north side of the island.

However, navigation in those years was not as precise, and there were other islands in this Santa Cruz group nearby: Tucopia (discovered by Quiros in 1606) is a half day's sail to the southwest; Vanikoro (La Pérouse) Island lies 100 miles to the west, followed by the remaining Santa Cruz's.

Thirty years after this voyage of the *Tonquin,* the United States Exploring Expedition under Charles Wilkes USN, which was a plan conceived and supported by Fanning himself, charted the Fijis and neighboring islands. Wilkes listed "Anuda and Mitre" Islands, but ironically his main works appear to be devoid of any reference to Fanning or to a "Tonquin Island." It is therefore probable that this name did not become officially accepted. Perhaps this was because Brumley did not have time on the voyage "to make an examination" or that he could not later establish this discovery as being original. Other explorers, much earlier, had sailed through the Santa Cruz group, including Meñdana with the ill-fated Spanish cruise of 1595; and also the La Pérouse expedition which disappeared in 1788, his vessels having foundered with all hands on the reefs of Vanikoro.

E. W. Giesecke
Olympia, Wash.
May 1969

THE NAVAL RECORD OF LIEUTENANT JONATHAN THORN

Born at Schenectady, New York, January 8, 1779, the eldest of fifteen children of Samuel Thorn and Helena Slyck Thorn.

Entered U.S. Navy April 28, 1800, aged 21 years, as midshipman.

Served with distinction in the war with Tripoli, where he was commended for bravery under fire.

Appointed acting lieutenant November 7, 1803, by order of Captain Edward Preble.

Returned to the U.S. with ship, U.S.S. Congress, December 5, 1805.

Appointed full lieutenant February 16, 1807, which was the highest rank he attained.

Appointed June 6, 1806, first commandant of the New York Navy Yard, where he served until July 15, 1807. At the time of this appointment he was only 27 years old and probably the youngest naval officer ever to be commandant of a U.S. Navy Yard, and the only man of his rank ever to so be appointed.

On May 18, 1810, furloughed to civilian life for two years to take command of the Tonquin, 290 tons, for a voyage to the Northwest Coast of America.

Death came to this courageous officer off the west coast of Vancouver Island in June, 1811. The exact date cannot be ascertained. The Tonquin left Astoria June 5th, proceding to Gray's Harbor to pick up an interpreter. The vessel made an undetermined number of stops on the way to its final anchorage. Thorn's death may have occurred as early as June 10 to 15. The earliest known record is from the log of the Hamilton, July 15, 1811, when there was 'hearsay of a ship taken to the south.' This is confirmed by an entry in the same log, "It seems to be true that a ship was taken at Wickaninnishes." This later entry was dated July 29, 1811, and it will be noted that the location was at Clayoquot and not Nootka. Some historians believe that the location for the destruction of the Tonquin was some miles north of this point, however several tape recordings by present day Indians give the location as Clayoquot. Several skin diving expeditions have searched for wreckage of the Tonquin but to date no evidence has been found.

Glen Adams

Summer, 1969

ATTACK AND MASSACRE OF CREW OF SHIP TONQUIN BY THE SAVAGES OF THE N.W. COAST

N Currier's Lith. N.Y.

VOYAGES

TO THE

SOUTH SEAS, INDIAN AND PACIFIC OCEANS,

CHINA SEA, NORTH-WEST COAST,

FEEJEE ISLANDS, SOUTH SHETLANDS, &c. &c.

WITH AN ACCOUNT OF THE

NEW DISCOVERIES MADE IN THE SOUTHERN HEMISPHERE,

Between the Years 1830—1837.

ALSO,

THE ORIGIN, AUTHORIZATION, AND PROGRESS OF THE FIRST

AMERICAN NATIONAL SOUTH SEA EXPLORING EXPEDITION

With Explanatory Notes relative to the Enterprise.

By EDMUND FANNING,

AUTHOR OF "FANNING'S VOYAGES."

Second Edition.

NEW-YORK:

WILLIAM H. VERMILYE.

1838.

TO

THE AMERICAN PEOPLE,

IN TESTIMONY OF HIS

HIGH ADMIRATION OF THEIR CHARACTER,

AS AN ENLIGHTENED NATION,

THIS VOLUME

IS MOST RESPECTFULLY DEDICATED,

BY

THE AUTHOR.

PREFACE.

It is with great diffidence that the author presents the following work to an enlightened public; still he is encouraged by the fact, that a previous volume on voyages, has met with indulgence and favour at their hands. He therefore deems it but justice to a generous public to state, that he has had the experience, both in the command and directive agency of upwards of seventy voyages, to those portions of our globe which are treated of in the course of this work. He would also state, that these voyages have not only been the means of bringing large amounts of wealth into our country and her national treasury, but have also opened and paved the way to many enterprising citizens to engage and succeed in the same lucrative trade.

The author has, to the best of his judgment, made selections of the most interesting and improving narratives of the voyages in which he has been concerned; and he flatters himself that the matter in these pages will not only be found entertaining, but that much information may be gathered relative to commercial trade, the whale and seal fishery, navigation, &c., and also the different seas, climates, habits and customs of the natives, lands and isles of the ocean.

The author having no pretensions to a literary education, and having enjoyed only the benefit of a village school, cannot but entertain the hope that the liberal and enlightened critic will suffer him and his work to pass unscathed, and that an indulgent public will make due allowance for inaccuracies of expression, while they can rely with the utmost confidence on the correctness of the facts stated.

CONTENTS.

PART I.

PART II.

PART III.

PART IV.

PART V.

PART VI.

PART VII.

PART VIII.

APPENDIX.

PART I.

NARRATIVE OF THE VOYAGE OF THE SHIP HOPE, FROM NEW-YORK, TO THE FEEJEE ISLANDS, IN THE SOUTH PACIFIC OCEAN, AND TO CHINA, UNDER THE COMMAND OF CAPTAIN REUBEN BRUMLEY, WITH THE DIRECTIVE AGENCY* OF THE AUTHOR, IN THE YEARS 1806—1808.

CHAPTER I.

Leave New-York—Departure from Sandy Hook—A gale—Tremendous foaming sea—A mountainous sea breaks on board ship—Loss of stern boat—Cape de Verde Islands—Governor's conduct—Depart from St. Jago.

Aug. 31*st*, 1806.—Having received the pilot on board, and hoisted our anchor, and being all in high spirits, our trig little ship stood down the bay. We passed the Narrows, gained an offing without Sandy Hook, and discharged the Pilot. At the same time, our good friends, with their warmly-expressed wishes for an agreeable and fortunate voyage, took their leave. Our little bark filled away under a cloud of canvass, and we took our departure from Sandy Hook Light.

* See Fanning's Voyages, p. 328

Sept. 3d.—In latitude 40° 18′ N. we were met by a heavy gale from the eastern board, which obliged me for safety to cause the ship to be hove-to under her storm sails. The gale was accompanied with a mountainous sea, breaking and showing its dashing, white-crowned foam. At 8, A. M, one of those turbulent neighbours, of a mountain size, dashed its white-capped foam on board, and gave our good ship a complete drenching and a giant thump, taking away with it our stern boat from its davids, much to our regret. We received no other damage of consequence. At 10, A. M., the violence of the gale abated, and it gradually moderated by 2, P. M., to only a strong breeze, veering round to the S.S.W. We now met with the usual weather, at the intervals of passing time—clear and cloudy, rain and sunshine, fresh gales and calms, which accompanied us until the 14th of October, when, at 11, A. M., we had sight of the Isle Sal, one of the Cape de Verdes, bearing W.S.W., distant 13 leagues. Our variation at this time, was 5° west. At meridian, the Isle Sal bore from us, W. by N., distant 11 leagues; our latitude, by sun's altitude, at same time, was 16° 48′ north. Soon after we had sight of Bonavista Island; and, on continuing our course to the southward, the Isle of Mayo soon appeared in view. At sun rising, on Thursday, 16th, we had a view of the Island of St. Jago, the largest of this group, bearing N.W. by W., 4 leagues distant. At half-past 7, A. M., the ship being then near and abreast the mouth of Port Praya harbour, I despatched Messrs. Brown and S. Coles, in a whale-boat, to procure, on shore, some small stock, with refreshments of vegetables and fruit. On our officers landing, agreeably to their instructions, they immediately waited on His Excellency the Governor, to obtain permission to accomplish their errand. His Excellency, on first words, demanded five Spanish dollars, as his landing fee, for the officers steping on shore on his island. This demand being satisfied, the Governor then said, he could not grant any permission to procure supplies, until he had perused and inspected the ship's sea letter ; which obliged Mr. Brown, maugre all his solicitations and persuasive arguments, to despatch his brother officer, Mr. S. Coles, to the ship for said letter. Captain Brumley, not expecting his boat so soon to return, was now making a lengthy board off with his ship, to enable her, during his boat's absence, to hold her ground to windward, against the strong lee current, while he gave his officers time to complete their purchases, &c., on shore. This gave Mr. Coles a long pull before the ship discovered his signal. On coming alongside the ship,

Captain B. being informed of the demand of His Excellency, instantly gave orders to tack ship in shore. When again near and abreast of the harbour's mouth, he despatched the boat, with Messrs. Napier and Coles, with the ship's sea letter, to Mr. Brown. At meridian, the Fort at the harbour of Port Praya, bore N. N.W., distant 3 leagues, when our latitude was, by good altitudes, 14° 54′ N. At 2, P. M., the ship being close in abreast the mouth of the bay, a signal was hove out for the boat to return on board. At 5, P. M., she came along side, and, as soon as she was hoisted in, all sail was made, with a fine, brisk trade-breeze, causing our good little ship to divide the surface of Neptune's element, in her quick rate of departure, from this unfeeling and disobliging Governor, as well as to fast widen the distance between her and the shore of his island.

Mr. Brown now reported to me that this *humane* and friendly magistrate to suffering seamen in serious want, would not permit him to purchase any small stock of pigs, fowls, &c., but only the very limited number of cocoa-nuts and oranges which the boat brought off. Even these were by much solicitation and persuasion permitted to be purchased, at a high rate, of particular persons pointed out to make the sale by his Excellency. At the same time, the market was well stocked, and persons from the country were humbly begging to be permitted to sell their articles, at a much lower rate.

At 6, P. M., Port Praya bore N.N.E., distant 5 leagues, when we took our departure, steering to the southeastward, to cross the equator for the Indian ocean.

CHAPTER II.

Violent squalls—A water-spout—Its terrific threatenings and passing roar—Shoals of whales—Cross the equinoctial line—Cape Aguillas' Bank—Gannets, and other birds —A white squall—Many whales seen.

As we progressed south, we experienced much unpleasant weather, accompanied with heat, thunder and lightning, and heavy squalls of wind and rain, near to, and north of the Equinoctial Line. In about the latitude of 6° north, during a violent squall of wind and heavy rain, we were obliged, for safety, to clew down the top-sails, and put the ship before the wind. In the midst of our anxiety for the safety of our masts, to our sudden surprise, a terriffic, sea-serpent-like-shaped water-spout appeared in view, coming at a rapid rate, as if direct in chase of us. Our ship was yawed broadly off, to endeavour to get out of its way, and of its threatened destruction ; and, although she was now going through the water at a very swift rate, still, in its passing, rushing roar, it seemed, to our dread, to be only about a cable's length clear of our ship, giving us only a soaking drench as it passed on. Surely these mighty, whirl-wind water-pyramids, connecting, in one giant link, as it were, the heavens with the sea, must be an awful evidence to man of the wonderful power of that almighty and good Being, who made, directs, and governs all. In about the latitude of 5° north, we saw numbers of shoals of whales, gambolling and thrashing about in their element, most probably after the small fry. At this situation, we had 11° west variation, which decreased as we advanced and crossed the line, in longitude 20° 32′ 15″ west, into south latitude. In latitude 2° 18′ south, we had 10° west variation. On Monday, 24th December, being in latitude 36° 37′ south, the sea-water became coloured, when we judged ourselves on the edge of the bank off Cape Aguillas. We saw seals playing around in the water, and many oceanic birds cutting the air on their wing, in all directions—such as gannets, albatrosses, cape pigeons, and mother carys. Our variation at this time was, per amplitude, 26° 10′ west. On the 27th, at 1, A. M., during a pleasant breeze and weather, our ship was suddenly struck by a white squall, which blew with great violence; and it was with much difficulty, so sudden was its approach, that we saved our sails. This severe squall was the more remarkable, as the moon was then shining, being near her full. The heavens were thinly overcast, with small white clouds, forming, what is called by seamen, a mackerel sky. There was, in fact, at the time, more the appearance of a calm, than of squalls. It, however, blew violently for about two hours, when it suddenly shifted from W. N. W. to the S. W., and moderated to only a fresh breeze.

Monday, January 5th, 1807.—Our latitude was 36° 24′ south; longitude, by lunar observation, 52° 16′ 30″ east. Hereabouts we saw many whales playing around in their element, to all appearance much delighted; these monsters of the deep having been our neighbours so frequently of late, I should think it good whaling-ground here. The oceanic birds, of various kinds, continued daily to accompany us; and, for four or five days past, our ship has been making only moderate way. Our variation now was, 24° 10′ west. Since our arriving to above the latitude of 30° south, we had variable winds from all points of the compass, and, as the sailors remark, all sorts of weather.

CHAPTER III.

Islands of Amsterdam, and St. Paul's—Whales and seals—Sea scurvy—New Holland—White beach—Columns of smoke—Remarkable rock—Cape Chatham.

Thursday, January 29th, 1807.—We had sight of Amsterdam Island. At meridian it bore E. by N., distant 14 leagues. Previous to our departure, I made the centre of Amsterdam to be, by good meridian altitudes and lunar sights, in latitude 38° 37′ south; longitude, 77° 17′ east, from London. As we passed these two Islands of Amsterdam and St. Paul's, many whales and seals were seen, as also numerous birds of various kinds.

February 4th.—At noon, our latitude was 37° 44′ south; longitude, 90° 53′ 20″ east, and the variation 13° 30′ west. We had now the third man on the sick list, with the sea scurvy; and although I restricted them to a diet of only raw potatoes and onions, in vinegar, with boiled rice and molasses, yet, if there was any change, the patients rather grew daily worse.

Monday, the 16th.—At noon, our observations placed the ship in latitude 33° 44′ south; longitude, 114° 01′ 20″ east; variation, at same time, was 7° 45′ westerly. We had now a brisk breeze from S. by E., with hazy weather. At 6, P. M., that welcome sound to the way-worn mariner, after a long passage, of "Land, ho!" by the look-out aloft, was heard. It proved to be the coast of New-Holland, bearing, by compass, E. by S. about 5 leagues distant, and had the appearance of islands, which were soon perceivable from the deck. We now steered along its coast; and, at 11, A. M., we were abreast of a very remarkable white, sandy beach, which bore E.S.E., distant 6 leagues; at which time the southernmost land in sight, bore S.E. ½ E., distant 8 leagues. Large columns of smoke were now seen from several parts of the land, which was of a moderate elevation, and apparently well wooded; the ascending smokes we supposed were made by the natives, on the appearance of our ship, and gave an evidence that this part of New Holland was thickly inhabited. With a favourable breeze, we continued sailing to the eastward, along the coast, and, at daylight, on the 17th, we had again a sight of the land—a point bearing N.E. ½ E., distant 9 leagues. Soon after, the look-out, at the mast head, sung out, "Sail, ho!" Not thinking to meet here with any thing like a ship, we were much surprised. As we advanced, however, and the sun got up, it proved to be a rock. The weather, when it was first seen, was very hazy; but it now lighted up, and gave a better and more extensive view. At 6, A. M., Cape Chatham (so named by Vancouver) was seen, bearing E. ½ N., distant 7 leagues. Our ship was now at no great distance from what was first, by the lookout, taken for a sail, but which now showed itself plainly to be a large rock, about a mile in circumference. Its E.N.E. side is nearly perpendicular; its W.N.W. side sloping down to the water. In the direction of E. by N. from it, lies a small rock, over which the sea breaks continually. Its distance from the large rock, or islet, is about half a mile. This rock bears from Cape Chatham, N. 79° W., distant thirteen or fourteen miles. This remarkable islet, not being mentioned in Vancouver, or Turnbull's Voyages, or on any chart in my possession, I concluded it to be a new discovery, and called it after our first sight and surprise on its appearance, *Sail Rock*, and placed it in latitude 34° 59′ south, and longitude, 116° 20′ east, and about nine miles off shore from the nearest land of the coast. At 8, A. M., Cape Chatham bore east, 4 leagues distant, and appeared plainly to be detached from the main land by means of a passage, apparently navigable for vessels of a considerable burthen. This, it seems, Captain Vancouver did not ascertain, although his opinion was, as we have found it, and as I have here noted; and we therefore called it, *Hope Passage.* Large fires continued to be made on shore upon the upland, as we advanced along the coast, as also for several miles far in the interior; the blaze and smoke of these fires ascended very high. At meridian, Cape Chatham bore N.W. by W. ¾ W., distant 5 leagues, when the ship's latitude was 35° 08′ south.

CHAPTER IV.

Cape Howe—King George III. Sound—Bald Head—Newly invented still for obtaining fresh water from that of the ocean—Van Diemen's Land—The Mew Stone—The Feathered Tribe—Amphibious Bird—Anchor at Botany Bay—Sydney Cove—Governor's humane and honourable conduct—Contrast between his and that of St. Jago's—Doctor O'Conner—His humane feelings and kind attention to the sick—Landing the sick—Sea scurvy—Its singularity.

Wednesday, February 18th.—At daylight, Cape Howe was seen bearing N.N.E. ¾ E. distant 8 leagues, with the detached Island off the Cape, which bore E. by N. ¾ N. distant 5 leagues. The weather now soon became dark and thick, attended with a heavy gale of wind from the S.W. blowing in tremendous hard squalls, which made our horizontal view soon very limited, and caused us to take in and furl the topsails. It also shortly became prudent to haul off to the southward, and to reduce the canvass on the ship to her fore course, and storm staysails only; since, by the increasing violence of the gale, even with these limited sails, there was a heavy pressure which caused her by the sea rolling on to labour hard as she plunged through it. I, however, thought it necessary to carry this press on her to keep her from driving to the leeward of our intended port, King George the III. Sound, thinking we yet might have a chance to bring our ship at anchor in this port, if we could, during the gale, enable her to hold her ground, and it should soon moderate. At 8, A. M., we had sight of Bald Head, one of the chops of the above Sound, which was at this time the easternmost land in sight, bearing N by E. The distance, owing to the state of the weather, uncertain. At 9, A. M, the gale still increasing, I judged it best, our stock of water being now reduced to but five casks, to bear up and put the ship before the gale, preferring to endeavour to reach with all despatch, and to touch in at Port Jackson for the relief of our sick, and the necessary supplies of refreshments.

We therefore put the ship before the gale, and on squaring away, directed our course for Van Diemen's Land, and in thus deciding, prudence requiring it, each man, officers and all on board, were put on an allowance of two quarts of water each, per diem.

Wednesday, 25th.—The carpenter, an ingenious mechanic, with the aid of a musket barrel, on trial, succeeded in an invention, and rigged up a still at the galley, or cooking coppers, which produced to us, from the sea water, fifteen gallons of fresh water per 24 hours.

It would have been a great and very thankful relief to my mind, had we have been permitted to have come at anchor with our ship in the Sound, as I was especially anxious for the relief of our scorbutic patients. Our head cook was this day taken, or reported on the list, with this discouraging and spirit-killing disease, which not only added another to our invalid list, taken off duty, but one with whom it was very inconvenient to dispense. However, our good little ship was now ploughing her way over the surface of Neptune's element, and rapidly advancing on her course before the strong and fair gale.

Thursday, the 5th of March.—At 6, A. M, we were cheered by the look-out aloft with that ever-welcome sound of "Land, ho!" and very soon thereafter we had sight, from the deck, of the S.W. Cape of Van Diemen's Land, bearing per compass N.E., distant 11 leagues. At 11, A. M.,we had sight of the Islet, Mew Stone, bearing north, distant 5 leagues. At 5, P M., Swilley Island was also in sight, bearing N. E., and at the same time the Eddy Stone had come within our view, bearing N.E. by E., about 5 leagues distant. We were now accompanied by great numbers of the feathered tribe, of various kinds, flapping their pinions and sailing on the spread wing in every direction. That amphibious bird, the penguin, was also diving around us in Neptune's waving field of water, in shoals, or companies of hundreds. As our ship drew in nearer to terra-firma, we were also visited by land birds of various kinds, one of which resembled the pigeon hawk, and was of a dark brown colour.

At 6, A. M., Tasman's Head, the southernmost extremity of Wm. Pitt's Island, bore W. N.W., distant 8 leagues, when the northernmost land in sight bore N.N.W., 12 leagues distant. We now had clear, pleasant weather, with a moderate breeze from the south.

March 8th.—I was extremely anxious to get the ship into port, as our sick list with the scurvy had now increased to nine, who were unable to keep the deck, and the number was almost daily increasing. The refreshing fragrance from the land, as it came off to the ship with the flaws, had evidently an effect on even the worst of them.

I therefore in person kept a sharp attendance on the working and sailing the ship along the coast; and after passing many capes, headlands and islands, on the 16th of March we were gratified with the sight of Point Solander, bearing N.W., distant 10 miles, and likewise that of Cape Banks, bearing N.W. ¾ N., distant 4 leagues. On reaching abreast of the harbour of Botany Bay, we gave the signal for a pilot, by the discharge of a gun. At this time also sounded, and had bottom or ground at 63 fathoms, muddy with black sand, and specks.

On the 17th, at 1, P. M., a small sail boat hove in sight, standing out from Botany Bay, and steering for the Hope, which soon came alongside, and accommodated us with a pilot, who, on coming on deck, requested that his boat should be hoisted in, which request was complied with. The weather began now to put forth a very threatening appearance, the wind increasing to a strong gale, with a heavy sea. The pilot directed the ship to be tacked and to stand off shore, which was promptly done; and I must admit that his judgment proved correct;

for our ship was soon forced to come under close reefed topsails.

At 2, A. M., wore ship, and stood in again for the land. At 5, A. M., it having moderated, made all sail, steering in for the Bay ; and at 8, A. M., we most gladly came to anchor in Sydney Cove, Port Jackson, in 7 fathoms water. In a short time thereafter, two officers came on board as a guard, and were soon followed by Dr. Harris, the Naval Officer of that port, who delivered to me the established port regulations, orders, &c., for our guide during our stay here.

In the time we spent in working our ship from the southernmost cape or land down along the coast to this port, we experienced much heavy thunder and sharp, vivid lightning, with occasional heavy showers of rain, attended with gusts, or short gales. Much the same weather continued while we remained here in port, excepting now and then some short spells of clear weather, during which we had delightful pleasant days.

March 18*th.*—I had the honour of paying a visit and presenting my respects to His Excellency the Governor, whom I found to be truly a gentleman of honourable and humane feelings, and corroborating them by ready and noble acts, speaking volumes in meritorious credit to His Britannic Majesty, and to the character of that liberal nation under whom he holds his official station. He was entirely the opposite to the Governor of St. Jago, (Cape de Verdes,) for on my solicitation, he granted, with the most prompt readiness, liberty to land our sick on Garden Island, which was situated about a mile distant from our ship. He also gave permission to obtain every aid for their comfort, and enabled me immediately to engage Doctor O'Conner, a physician of first note and talent in his profession, to attend them while on the Island.

This disorder, the sea scurvy, is a very strange disease, as very soon after the patient is taken with it, he loses all spirits, and every disposition to action. Even any inclination to move at all has entirely vanished ; and when the limbs become much, or rather, as in some instances, enormously swelled, on pressing your thumb on the fleshy part, it will cause a deep indentation, as if done on a mass of putty, —which indentation will remain the same for hours, while the act causes no pain to the patient. It is singular how soon the earth, on placing the patient upon it, with a diet of fruit, vegetables, salads, &c., for his constant food, with the lightest and not luscious fresh meat soups, revives him, and fast recruits again his health. When advanced in the disease and weak from it, the very smell or scent of the land, or disembarking from the ship, very much affects them, even to frequent faintings.

Our sick, on landing, were, much to my consolation, now placed on a lovely green and comfortable situation, with the promise of their speedy recovery ; were all daily attended and supplied with a full allowance of fresh meat soups, fresh fish, vegetables, fruit, &c., and daily visited, with the most solicitous and humane feelings, by Dr. O'Conner, myself always accompanying him, to be certain that every article was furnished to secure their comfort and prompt recovery.

While here, we were very kindly and courteously treated by His Excellency the Governor, and His Majesty's officers ; and by their ready and obliging aid we completed our supplies of refreshments, wood and water. Our invalids having recovered, most of them to their duty, and all pronounced by the Doctor out of danger, they returned on board, free from any fear of their complaint returning soon again in going to sea. Our ship was therefore of course now prepared and got ready for sailing.

CHAPTER V.

Departure from Sydney—A strange ship—Macauley's and Curtis' Islands—Sunday Island—Numerous Birds and Fishes—Island of Tongataboo—Van Diemen's Road—Bad Anchorage—Directions in sailing among the Islands—Coral reefs—A strange ship appears—Strict inquiry of the natives for white persons among them.

Friday, April 3d, 1807.—Having paid my parting respects to His Excellency, with thanks for his kindness, and taken an adieu of His Majesty's officers and the gentlemen merchants, with whom an acquaintance had been made while here, we received our pilot on board, and orders were issued to weigh anchor, and proceed to sea. As soon as we had gained without the South Head, a strange ship was descried in the offing, and the pilot soon after took his leave of us, and proceeded to board the stranger, which was steering in for the port. At meridian, the South Head of Port Jackson bore W. by N., distant 9 leagues, from which we took our departure from the continent of New Holland, to proceed on our passage for Tongataboo, one of the Friendly Islands.

After a passage of ordinary winds and weather, without any remarkable incident occurring, on Sunday, the 19th, we had sight of Macauley's and Curtis' Islands. At noon, Macauley's Island bore N.E. ¾ E., distant 4 leagues; and our latitude at this time, by a good observation, was 30° 24′ S.; variation, 13° 5′ E. On the 20th, we had sight of Sunday Island. At meridian, its northernmost end bore N. by E. ½ E., distant 5 leagues, our latitude then being 29° 24′ S. Our ship was now surrounded by vast numbers of the feathered tribe; and, at the same time, were gambolling in their element around us numerous fishes of various sorts. We were not so fortunate, however, as to induce any one of them to take the bait on the hook. The largest, or giant kind, (whales,) we declined offering the baited hook to, believing it perfectly useless, and being somewhat acquainted with their mighty strength and quick motion; for should we offer and they incline to take the hook, we should, to a certainty, only have the "success of loss," (as Paddy would say,) to lose our hook, if not our line with it. Several rocks were now within our view, extending off from the south end of Sunday Island, and detached from it.

On the 26th, a very clear day, we had sight of Pylstart's Island, bearing W., distant 14 leagues; and on Monday, the 27th, at 5 P. M., we got sight of Eooa, or Middleburgh Island, bearing per compass N. by E. ½ E., distant 10 leagues. At 10, A. M., the long-wished-for Island of Tongataboo, or New Amsterdam, was in sight, bearing N.N.W., distant 8 leagues. It is very low land, and has, on first view, in clear weather, somewhat the appearance of a reef of rocks of a moderate height. We now bore away for this Island, and prepared all in order for the best defence by loading our carriage guns, &c. &c. As we sailed along its coast to the westward, when arrived opposite the Bay, and while working the ship into Van Diemen's Road, several canoes, containing numbers of the natives with the products of their Island for a barter trade, came off around our ship. Their variety for trade consisted of cocoa-nuts, bread-fruit, plantains, &c., for which we traded and bartered our riches, (so considered by them,) viz. pieces of old iron hoop, knives, needles, small looking glasses, beads, buttons, nails, &c. Having worked in on the bank near to the shore, we now, as expected, brought our ship at anchor, by letting drop the best bower anchor in 30 fathoms over a bed of coral and sand, very close in shore. Although we quickly and briskly paid out 90 fathoms of cable, the bank was so very steep, that she did not bring up, but soon dragged off of it, and shortly clear out, off soundings, when we in dull cheer hove up our anchor to its place on the bow again, and made sail under sad disappointment to regain the anchorage. However, on regaining our former position on the bank in the bay, I thought it best to keep the ship under way, on short tacks, as we were now surrounded by an additional number of canoes of all sizes, containing large swarms of natives, and carrying on a brisk trade for refreshments in hogs, vegetables, fruits, &c., which the Island seemed very bountifully to produce.

Directions.—After obtaining sight of Eooa, run down on the south side, when you will soon come in sight of Cattaw Island, and then Tongataboo; keeping as you advance all on the starboard hand, you may double round these islands, I believe close to the shore, as we saw no danger. I recommend, however, and it is highly important, that a *trusty officer*, while navigating here, be continually at the mast-head, on a good look-out for those coral reefs, (which seem, as it were, in these seas, to grow up in a night,) and rocks, but which with this caution can be seen at a reasonable distance and avoided, even if under the surface of the water, and no break over them. Van Diemen's Road is on the northwest part of

Tongataboo, and forms a small bay, or bend in the coast. On entering this road, I found a strong current setting on the west point or chop, which point is composed of a white sand, and extends off about two cables' length into the sea, very shoal. Be careful of borrowing too near in shore when in the road, as there will be found a swell or under tow continually heaving in shore.

We obtained here at Tonga, in barter with the natives, good rope and cinnet, made from the fibres of the cocoa-nut.

Thursday, the 30th.—At 8, A. M., a ship was descried in the eastern board, standing to the N.W., but shortly after she bore up for us, and proved to be the King George, of and from Port Jackson, bound also to the Feegees, James Akins, Commander, who very courteously offered to keep us company, and to work into the Road with us, with the like view to procure for his ship such provisions and refreshments as the Island afforded.

This day, with earnest zeal and attention, I improved in the endeavour to obtain all and every information relative to the melancholy fate of Captain Isaac Pendleton and his boat's crew, of the Union,* and with the view of re-

* See Fanning's Voyages, page 323.

lief, should there be any civilized person detained by the chiefs on Tongataboo, I made every inquiry also for any white persons, to ascertain if there was even a single one now remaining on the Island, but could not learn from the chiefs or natives that there was even one left. A vast number of the natives in crowds kept parading on the beach at every time while and when the ship was in the Road trading with those in the canoes

While here we experienced occasionally squalls of thunder and lightning, accompanied with exceeding thick and dark weather, with however some fair and pleasant intervals.

CHAPTER VI.

Departure from Tonga for the Feejees—Fatoa (or Turtle) Island—Dangers of the ship among the Feejee Archipelago—Most dangerous navigation—Caution of the Natives—Numerous groups of Islands—A Chief comes on board—Double canoes—King Tynahoa—Dignity of His Majesty—Description of his person—Lofty peaked mountain—Gorroo Chief—Boat excursion.

Sunday, May 3d, 1807.—Having engaged as pilots and interpreters a Tonga and a Feejee man, and having them now on board, we bore away; but the heart of the Tonga man failing him, he became unwilling to proceed. I therefore directed him to embark in a canoe that was near by, and return—which he gladly, to appearance, complied with.

We now, in company with the King George, took a final departure from Van Diemen's Road, which I place in latitude 21° 04′ south, and longitude 175° 18′ west. It being dark and squally through the night, we thereby parted company with the King George, and saw her not afterwards during our passage.

May 4th.—At 1, P. M., the appearance of the weather was very unpropitious, in the opinion of our Feejee pilot, to run for our small mark, (Turtle Island,) called by the natives Fatoa. We therefore close-reefed the topsails, and hauled the ship upon a wind, with her head to the southward. It now blowing a gale, with a tremendous sea running, our good ship laboured hard.

May 7th.—At 3, P. M., we got sight from aloft of Fatoa Island, bearing W. by S., distant 6 leagues. It yet blowing a gale from the northeastward, and being cloudy weather, attended with heavy squalls of wind and rain, accompanied with sharp lightning and thunder, and with a large irregular sea, the ship was still under close-reefed topsails and fore course.

Her latitude at this time was 19° 33′ south, and the variation 12° 20′ east.

May 15.—We now were blessed with settled pleasant weather, and also with a moderate trade wind from the E.N.E. At 2, P. M., we had sight of two islands; the largest was called by the Feejee Chief, our pilot, Honghare Levo, and bore (all our bearings are taken by compass) N. by W., distant 8 leagues. The small one was called by same authority Honghare Livi, and bore from us N.N.W., distant 7 leagues. At the same time, Turtle Island bore S.S.E. ½ E., distant 8 leagues. At 3, P. M. Falongaa Island was in sight, looking at this distance like two islands, bearing N.W. by W. ½ W., distant 5 leagues. I now hauled the ship up to weather Falongaa, and at half-past 5 P. M. saw to appearance through between Falongaa and Honghare Islands a passage. In that direction, also, four other islands came within our view: I now tacked ship to the eastward, to spend the night under short sail and tacks, keeping our ship as near as possible over the same ground or place during the night. In and during the evening, saw lights on shore at Falongaa. At 6, A. M., Honghare bore N.N.W. ½ W. when our ship was at this time 6 leagues distant from its N.W. end. At noon, its S.W. point bore N.W., distant 2 leagues:

at the same time, the west point of Folongaa bore N.W., distant 5 leagues. A reef extends off from the N.E. point of Honghare. Our latitude now by observation was 19° 21′ south.

May 16*th*.—Descried a canoe, under sail, coming out from Honghare, and steering for us. When she had arrived near by, I directed the ship to be hove-to; but no signs or persuasions, by myself or our pilot chief, could induce the natives in her to come on board. At 3, P. M., we had sight of Annamoohoa Island, bearing N.W., distant 6 leagues; at same time, the north point of Honghare bore E. by S., distant 4 leagues. A current sets through the passage between Annamoohoa and its opposite island. At 6, P. M., tacked ship to eastward, to spend the night, keeping the ship as near the spot of her present situation as possible; and a very disagreeable and most anxious night it was, to my mind. The weather being thick, and having very limited sea-room in which to manœuvre the ship, over a bottomless sea, between the islands, as may be judged, when morning came, and gave daylight to our aid, it made us sensible of our dangerous situation during the night just past. At 8, A. M., of this numerous group, eighteen islands were in sight. At this time, the N.E. end of Annamoohoa bore N.W. by N., distant 7 leagues. At 9, A. M., it falling calm, a masted canoe came alongside with a chief, accompanied by nine natives. The chief very willingly supplied us with all the yams, &c., brought off in his canoe, in barter for beads and buttons. Soon after he had taken his leave of us, a number of canoes came off from the islands to pay us a visit, and dispose of their vegetables and fruits. At noon, the centre of Hengasaw Livo bore N.E., distant 4 leagues. Thus, in the sailors' phrase, ends this 24 hours, calm as a clock. Our latitude now, at noon, was, by observation, 19° south, and the variation was, 10° 30′ east.

May 18*th.*—This day we were visited by several large double war-canoes, as well as others of different make and form, containing numerous jabbering natives, who viewed the ship with wonder and surprise, and seemingly utter astonishment, not having seen here such a floating island (as they called her) before, and bringing with them a good supply for barter with us, of excellent yams, &c. A barter trade was now very briskly carried on, for the shining riches (in their estimation) on board our ship. Among the natives, Labooulyi, the Feejee chief and pilot, that came with us from Tongataboo, met with his relatives, and took his leave of us, in one of the double canoes. At 10, A. M., Tynahoa, the Grand Chief and

King of all these islands, in a very large, gaily decked double canoe, and truly brilliantly adorned after their manner, and show of state, with carved work, &c. &c., attended, in addition, by his nobles in royal state and movement, came alongside the ship. From the gangway I invited his royal person on board; which invitation, His Majesty, after causing to be passed on board his welcoming presents to me, consisting of a fat shote, yams, cocoa-nuts, &c., readily complied with; and came promptly on the ship's deck, to all appearance in full confidence, without the least show of fear or hesitation. He then moved about with his two attendant chiefs from this to that object with all the readiness his inquiries would admit; viewed, and closely inspected every article, fixture, &c., and inquired the use or purpose of the form and construction of the ship, with her equipments for war, accommodations, &c. &c. He scrutinized with minuteness, and with much ease and dignity in his movements. At the same time, he was earnest in his inquiries concerning the use of this and that thing or article. His Majesty's personal appearance was truly noble. He was six feet three inches in height, and well proportioned every way; had a pleasant, but commanding countenance, and was about forty years of age. After being satisfied with viewing the ship, &c., and receiving from me some small shining trinkets as my return present, but, to him, sufficiently and satisfactorily valuable as a present to royalty, he took his leave, inviting me to pay him a visit at his royal residence on the island. He embarked, seating his royal person under the canopy on the platform or deck of his magnificent double war-canoe. The accompanying fleet moved from us in great state for the shore, and landed at Nahow, one of his principal residences. His Majesty, however, before parting, gave to me a promise to return on board again in the morning, and accompany us in the ship down to Gorroo Island.

May 21st—At 8, A. M., we had sight of a very lofty, spiral, or peaked mountain, on the main island, Toconroba, which bore N. by W. ½ W , distant 7 leagues. At 10, A. M., a large canoe came off from Gorroo, with a chief, who, after tendering and receiving presents, at his own desire, remained on board. I now despatched Mr. Brown, the first officer, in a whale-boat, well armed, and manned by six good men, with provisions for two days, to explore the seaboard and outer bounding coral reef for the passage for our ship to our intended port, at the King's main island of Toconroba, (subsequently named Sandal Wood Bay.) Our latitude, at situation of ship at this time, was 17° 27′ south.

CHAPTER VII.

King again visits the ship—Freedom of His Majesty—A Royal Present—Brisk Trade—Ship surrounded by War-Canoes, with Armed Warriors—Expected Battle—Cannibal war-yells—The Leader Chief—Signal of Retreat—Warriors depart—Direction Island—Dangerous situation of the Ship—Three Mountains—The Sea Wall Reef—Narrow Passage—Rapid Current—Coral Reefs—Handsome Young Chief—Intricate Navigation, danger of—Boarding-Netting—Sandal Wood Cargo—Treaty with the King—His Majesty's Treasury Chest—Grand Council—Good Faith of the King—Articles of Trade.

May 22d.—The King, agreeably to his promise yesterday, now came on board, and, to show his confidence in us, his royal person was attended by only one chief and six native canoe men. As a first-rate royal present, His Majesty now presented me with a very large, fat boar hog, for which I made him a satisfactory return. After granting permission to his native subjects to enter on a free and brisk trade with us, for refreshments, in hogs, yams, &c., in barter for our valuable riches of shining metal buttons, small looking-glasses, glass beads, &c., His Majesty took his leave, and returned on shore.

May 24th.—At 11, A. M., a fleet of large, double war-canoes came off to the ship, from Nyri Island. This island was now in revolt, and at war with King Tynahoa, as His Majesty had previously informed me. One of these canoes led the van, and appeared to have the commanding chief on board, surrounded by other chiefs on her platform-deck. By their manœuvres, as they surrounded the ship, we judged that they had something important immediately in view, of a war-like cast. As their conduct was by no means altogether pleasing, or even friendly, and, as there appeared in this one canoe upwards of a hundred warriors, and in all the others a like number, in proportion to their size, it was plainly to be seen that they were well armed, after their manner, with spears, war-clubs, battle-axes, bows and arrows. Their canoes were all under sail, as well as paddles; and, after sailing and paddling round and round the ship, with, at same time, continued shouts, war-whoops, and cannibal yells—with grimaces and movements of body and limbs, showing, in their way, unfriendly actions and intentions, they now and then pointed to the ship's carriage-guns, and imitated with their voice, their explosion. The ship's battery was all this time kept ready and clear for action, each gun being loaded with a round shot and langrage, with matches burning, and every man wide awake at his station. After some time spent thus, in sailing around the ship, the commanding chief placed his war-canoe a few yards directly ahead, and in the way of our ship, and hauled down his sail. His men lay on their paddles, thinking, as it appeared, by thus doing, to drop his canoe alongside, and board us ; but as the ship was under some way, and observing his intentions, I instantly directed her to be given a broad yaw off. This immediately brought our guns and broadside to bear fairly on them and, in this way, we passed them, without any discharge, as we were acting only on the defensive. As the success of our voyage, and the safety of our absent boat, was constantly on my mind, as well as a deep reluctance to destroy life, I was determined not to commence the battle, but to act wholly on the defensive. They then used their paddles after us, keeping close under our stern, and insisting on making fast their rope to the ship. This we decidedly forbade and opposed, and effectually prevented without a fight. In the mean while, the rest of these large war-craft, with their crowd of armed warriors, breaking the air with their horrid war-yells, kept sailing and paddling around the ship, within pistol-shot distance, keeping up constantly their terrific war-whoops. They appeared to watch sharply all our motions, and those of their leader, at our stern. In this most trying and anxious situation, we were kept for the space of two hours; when, on a signal from their chief, their hideous war-yells ceased, and the whole fleet made sail at once, steering back from whence they came, to the Island of Nyri. Their departure gave to me, and I think to all on board, a feeling of relief. We were glad to be rid and clear of such a horrid, cannibal set of threatening visitors, without being forced into slaughtering measures in self-defence, which, as already observed, I was extremely anxious, in our situation, to avoid, as our worthy first officer, and six excellent seamen, absent in our boat, might, in such event, have been cut off and massacred. Any warlike measure, or act, would also very likely operate much against us, in relation to our errand, as we were now in the neighbourhood of our destination, where we expected to procure, in barter, our cargo of sandal wood, &c.

May 25th.—At 10, A. M., to our joy and relief, Mr. Brown, the first officer, returned on board from his exploring cruise, having been absent from the ship four days. During this time, we constantly kept the light signals out throughout the nights for him; and it may truly be presumed no small weight of anxiety existed on my mind during his absence.

On the 26th, at 8, A. M., saw a small island, which I called, and very appropriately, Direction Island, (not having learned the native name of it,) as it was situated directly in the range of the ship's passage through the outer main reef, and bore N.W. ½ N., distant two leagues.

May 28th.—Experienced a heavy gale and squally weather through the night; but it moderated to a light breeze at near daylight. As the morning light broke and lit up, it discovered to us the very dangerous situation of the ship, caused by the currents, as well as the gale, so near the shore, that we had hardly room to bring the ship about, and keep clear of being wrecked. However, on promptly well-manning our sweeps in her aid, we succeeded in bringing her in stays and about, with her head off from this dreaded, rocky shore, and, to appearance, at one time, of certain shipwreck on it. We were much aided and assisted in effecting our escape, by the alert working of our fast sailing little ship. The great relief our escape gave to me from shipwreck, on this wild, rocky, savage coast, can be judged, I think, only by a commander with the like charge, who has escaped from a like situation, and from the danger of being wrecked on a cannibal shore. The weather clearing up soon after, gave us a sight of Direction Island, when we wore ship and stood in towards it, for the passage. This island is a good mark to the mariners for the channel through the sea wall reef. Three very remarkable mountains were now within our view, over another island, bearing N.N.W., and the remarkable sharp, spiral mountain, on Toconroba, bore N. by W. At 11, A. M., I despatched Mr. Brown in a boat, who, in his exploring cruise, had discovered and sounded it out, to lay as a buoy mark in the passage through the outer main reef. At this time, Direction Island bore E. by N. ¾ N., distant 5 leagues. Mr. Brown having soon made the signal of his boat's situation in the channel, we bore the ship away under her fore-course and three topsails, with a brisk trade breeze, and every officer and man at his station. In about an hour, our good ship had passed safely through the reef, by the channel, where the boat lay, and which I judged to be only about fifteen yards wide, from side to side, or from rocks to rocks, of this sea-bound reef. The breadth here of this coral reef, I judged to be about two cables' length; we found the tide or current running very rapidly through the pass. After our ship was through, we hauled her up N. by E.; but our course soon became variable, on account of the many patches of shoal coral reefs, and rocks just under the surface of the sea-water ; these could be timely and plainly seen by the officer on the look-out aloft, and cunning our direction in the course for the ship. Our course mainly, from the narrow pass through the sea wall reef to Booje, our first anchorage, was about N. by E., and the distance about 7 leagues. We brought the ship at an anchor, with the small bower, at Booje, in 13 fathoms water, over a bottom of fine black sand : a low, sandy beach, with a grove of cocoa-nut-trees, and a native village, bearing E.N.E., distant half a mile. This anchorage I subsequently named Sandal Wood Bay and Road. With all precaution, we now bent the sheet-cable, and shackled the chain-cables to their anchors on the bows, as being in readiness and prepared for the worst event, and moored our ship with the stream anchor. Our latitude, at this anchorage, was 16° 58′ south. Soon after bringing our ship here at anchor, a trig built and very handsome young chief came alongside, in an uncommonly neatly built Tongataboo double canoe. He came without hesitation on board, and promptly presented me with several hundred fine cocoa-nuts as a welcome present ; in return for which, and

5

his free sociability, I made him a present of a proper return. He had been some time from Tonga; and his bold, but very neatly and highly-ornamented and carved-work craft, showed, incontestably, that they make their sea-voyages, at least thus far, in these double canoes. I cannot here sufficiently express my thankfulness to the Great Preserver of all, for his protection of those "who go down to the sea in ships, and do business in great waters," and especially since, notwithstanding our way has been very full of innumerable dangers, for having safely arrived here. The relief given to my mind and feelings, by our arrival at anchor, after so many, and so tedious, laborious, and very anxious scenes passed during those several days and nights among those islands, working our ship along in the most dangerous and intricate navigation, between these islands, that can be conceived. In these passages, there are innumerable scattering coral reefs; and, in fact, it will likewise generally be found the case, that without the outer verge of the wall sea bound reefs, no bottom, by soundings, is to be had or found with the lead, even at the distance of only two or three cables' length from its verge; therefore no anchorage is to be had or expected, as none is to be found. In addition, the sea, with its mountain billows, is usually breaking in massy foam and giant force; and the currents are irregular, and frequently of great force; the wind, at intervals, blows strong gales, dark and squally; still there are spells of clear, pleasant weather, but they happen mostly in the day time. The winds, during a great part of the time, were, when regular, of the trades, blowing from the eastern board, but at times variable, and, in hard squalls, generally followed by a calm. To make the task more severe, and the burthen heavier to a commander, we were, much of the time, and during the day in particular, surrounded by numerous canoes, with swarms of natives, keeping up the constant evidence before our eyes, that if we should be wrecked, immediate massacre was the destiny of all on board. After having safely performed this dangerous navigation, through this Archipelago, during the term of such a number of days, being our own pilots, and without charts, I think all must admit, that we would be likely to feel thankfully fortunate in bringing our ship thus safely into port, at anchor, and that all on board would be relieved. We leave it to the magnanimity of the general reader to give to us the credit we merit in its performance.

Some of the islands of this group are of moderate elevation; but others are very mountainous; several with lofty, spiral, or sugar-loaf peaks; others with round summits, and thickly wooded tops. The author would ask the liberty here to remark, that he has ever made it a permanent rule, not only to caution captains never to suffer over two or three principal chiefs, and their few attendant natives, (as those chiefs will always bring their attendants) to come on deck, at one and the same time; but also to have all the vessels ever sent out under their directive agency, and bound to those seas, on these voyages of barter-trade, among these children of nature, to be well fitted and armed, with the precaution of a boarding-netting made of rattling-stuff, and small iron chains, that a passage for a person might not be easily cut through its meshes. This should be attached to the ship's railing of cover at their quarters, and go entirely around the ship, and out on the sides of her bowsprit, to the fore-stay; and be so deep, as to admit tricing up, when among the savages, to twelve or fifteen feet above the rail. It being thus fitted, when the boarding-net is triced up, the ship's quarters and decks are encircled, if it may be so termed, similar to a highly fenced yard, so that not any person can enter or come on board the ship's deck, except at the pass, by the armed sentry at the gangway, and by the immediate permission of the officer in charge of this station. Sentries on guard are, or should be, at such times, always set on the tafferel, and on the heel of the bowsprit, to watch and observe all that is passing among the natives around the ship. With all these precautions, there is little danger; as when they are thus constantly prepared, and can all be put in requisition in a moment's warning, there is then little to fear while among those savages. The author has, thus prepared, at such time, had his ship surrounded by thousands of the natives, even in clusters, as it were, like a flock of birds on a tree, hanging on around, and on the sides of his ship, without the boarding-netting, and chattering their lingo, and observing all the movements of those on the ship's decks; still no unpleasant occurrence has ever caused the shedding of blood by the vessels under his charge.

The Hope being now in Sandal Wood Road, thus moored and prepared, and under her very judicious and vigilant commander, with our usual good discipline, we procured, at and off from Toconroba Island, her cargo; being the first, by Americans, of sandal wood, &c., from this group, without any unpleasant occurrence, or the least difficulty with the chiefs or inhabitants. At the same time, loaded an English vessel, on freight for Canton. In addition, engaged, in a treaty with the King, a cargo of wood, to be prepared and piled up on the small island near our present anchorage. This cargo was to be ready in eighteen moons (months) for any other ship belonging to the same owners ;* and by this treaty the King likewise engaged to cause the sandal wood trade to be tabooed (prohibited) from all other vessels procuring it, or taking any of it away from the islands. This unusual success by treaty, was mainly effected thus, as related to the author :—Their first officer, Mr. Brown, had become a great favourite, and the adopted son of the King, and, by living the greatest part of his time at His Majesty's residence, had learned to speak the Feejee language, so as to hold a conversation with the chiefs and natives, without an interpreter, or with little difficulty, which greatly pleased them all, and zealously attached His Royal Majesty to him. Captain Brumley, through this influence, was able to effect this treaty. Its conditions were as follows :—The Captain was to cause to be made by his carpenters, for the King, a large chest for his treasury, fourteen feet in length, with several apartments, and a separate lid to each apartment,

* Was subsequently taken to China by ship Tonquin.

with a padlock* to each apartment lid. This treasury chest, or reservoir, was engaged by the captain to be filled with an assortment of our articles of trade, to be selected by the King and his attendant chiefs, after the chest should be finished, and painted in a variety of high and gaudy colours; when thus finished, this grand treasury chest was placed in the palace, in a room designated and prepared for it, when each division was filled with suitable articles, of an assortment selected by His Majesty, &c., chiefs' wives and family; and then, when so filled, a new padlock was placed on each lid; the keys, tied in a bunch by a high-coloured silk ribbon, adorned with various coloured beads attached to it, and handed to His Majesty. The treaty was then considered as ready for ratification: and the reader may be assured, by what is represented, that, in the opinion of the author, the great Napoleon never felt better, in greater dignity, or in more importance, immediately after one of his greatest victories, than

* Mr. Brown had learned His Majesty the art of locking and unlocking a padlock, which much delighted his royal person, indeed almost to ecstasy; and he, in his exultation, now affirmed, that not any chief could inspect, or look at his great treasure, without his knowledge and permission. In fact, not one of them possessed ingenuity enough to unlock it, even should the key be put into their hand.

did His Royal Majesty Tynahoa, on receiving this bunch of keys. All the chiefs shouted by royal signal, and declared him to be now the greatest and richest monarch in their world, and were followed by a shout of thousands of the natives, that seemed to shake their island. A grand council of chiefs was now called, and ordered to assemble forthwith. They promptly assembled in the area, on the green lawn, in the cool shade, and under their valuable bread-fruit trees, in front of the King's palace; being thus met in council, His Majesty in the centre, on an elevated seat, after a few rapid speeches delivered by several of the chiefs in rotation, in their true native and uncivilized manner and actions, all tending to the blazing forth the great power and riches of their monarch, and how soon he would now conquer all the islands in their world; on a green branch being handed by the King, in person, to the captain, and Captain B. receiving it, the treaty was then considered ratified, and to be kept sacred by both parties. The council being dismissed by His Majesty, broke up, every one going his own way home, after repairing, in apparently perfect happiness, to the feast prepared by order of the King—consisting of roasted hogs, yams, bread-fruit, &c., and satisfying their wild and voracious appetites. Hereafter it will be seen, in the Tonquin's voyage, with what good faith this royal monarch, over an uncivilized mass of beings, and his chiefs and nobles in council, kept this treaty, and finally fulfilled it, as the result will prove, in such good faith as would be very commendable in any civilized monarch. The chiefs evidently, on departing, moved off in new and additional pride of carriage, and they certainly now considered their King by far the most powerful and wealthy monarch in all the Pacific ocean.

Our articles of trade here were, first, sperm-whales' teeth, of all sizes; but the larger, the more valuable in their estimation, as they were considered the highest emblem or mark of royal honour and favour. After the tooth was highly polished, a small hole was drilled through the larger end to hang it on the breast, by a ribbon or chord passed round the neck. The next article most valued by them were tokas, made by the armourer, at his forge; they being, in shape or form, merely the blades of adzes and hatchets, without an eye for the helve formed to them. In the room of the eye part, it was made to suit their notion, so as to be lashed to the helve or handle with a strong line, made from the fibres of the palm-tree. Glass bottles, either wine, porter, or square, were next in repute; high coloured calicoes;

looking-glasses of all shapes, and small sizes; bright metal buttons; needles of different sizes; iron spikes and nails; pieces of old iron-hoop, cut to the length of four to five inches; with a general assortment of ironmongery, principally cutlery, with iron tinned spoons. These composed the assortment of our articles of trade at the Feejees, at this time.

The invoice of articles of trade put on board the Hope, when she sailed on this voyage from New-York, by which the above purchases and bargains were made and completed, did not amount to but little more than nine hundred dollars. This sandal wood (being one of the articles procured in this trade, as to profit of a fair rate to judge by) brought, at that time, in the Canton market, about thirty cents the pound. Out of this, about one-third of the amount of the proceeds of a cargo was paid into the United States' treasury, on duties on the China goods, obtained in exchange for it in Canton. Thus vast amounts have, by vessels under the command and directive agency of the author, been, by the Pacific and China trade, brought into the American national treasury.

CHAPTER VIII.

Author's rule of trade in the prohibition of fire-arms—Natives of the Feejee Islands—Their cannibalism—Manner of obtaining sandal wood—Music to the natives in the wood-saw—Great number of the natives as the ship departs—Affection and attachment of the King to the first officer, Mr. Brown—His Majesty's parting with him—Union Massacre Passage—Alarm by the sudden discovery of the ship in shoal water—Departure from Feejees, and voyage to China—Crossing Equator twice—Equatorial currents—Discovery of Hope Island—Phillipine Islands—Their beautiful green appearance—Arrival at Canton—Sail for sweet home—Arrival at New-York.

The author would here beg leave to remark that, during his command and directive agency, in all the voyages of traffic with these children of nature, he has ever insisted that, when fire-arms, powder and ball, with other of the civilized destructive instruments of war, were demanded and peremptorily insisted on by the chiefs, in barter, to quit their trade sooner than to comply; as there is not a doubt but that these, to them new and destructive instruments, after they and their neighbours have come in possession of some of them, have been the cause of much bloodshed and massacre.

The natives of the Feejee Islands are, beyond question, cannibals, and even consider their roasted enemies as among their choicest feasts. Mr. Brown, being so much with the King, on one occasion, when an expedition of warriors had just returned from battle and victory, at Nyri, obtained over the Nyri Island natives, and were come with their victorious fleet of war-canoes, at the landing on the bank of the river, discovered among them a large double canoe having, on her deck platform, the bodies of some twenty or more slain enemies. After the King had selected two of the best fed and plumpest, of about twenty years of age, he directed them to be taken away to his residence, by his attendants, to be dressed and roasted for his conquering feast. His Majesty then divided, by lot, the remaining number among his principal chiefs; which were, in turn, by their attendants, taken away with the like directions.

We remained here in Sandal Wood Bay, at Toconroba Island, with our ship, trading for and procuring sandal wood, &c., until we not only loaded our own ship, the Hope, but also an English vessel we met here, that touched for refreshments, with a cargo on freight for Canton. We also paid, as per treaty, for a second cargo, for which a ship was to be sent; and made every necessary arrangement with the king for placing this second cargo of wood in the treaty as follows, viz: It was to be cut down, and then brought from the mountains during our eighteen moons' absence, and to be cut at right lengths as per sample, deposited with His Majesty, shaved and piled on the small island near the harbour, or road, where our ship was now moored at anchor.

Our manner while here of obtaining the sandal wood, was thus:—On concluding a bargain with the king (the whole of this article being royal property) for a certain quantity, to be delivered by a stipulated day, at the landing place, on the bank of the river, he would direct a chief to take his men, fifty, more or less in a gang, as the case required, proceed up the mountain, cut down such trees as should be selected by our men from the ship, and bring them trunk and limbs to the landing. The chief dared not for his life but be punctual in performing and accomplishing his task by the time agreed on. With this gang is sent one of the ship's crew, to select the large and sound trees, and, in charge of the saws, axes, and grind-stone, and to direct the sawing down the trees as close to the ground as possible. This sawing off the body with the cross-cut saw, bringing the tree down from the stump, was a highly favourite part of the work, and was fre quently severely disputed for between the natives, owing to the exquisite and delightful music to them, in the ringing of the saw. In fact, at times, they would dispute so earnestly abou whose turn it was, as to come to a raging grapple with each other. It frequently required the authority and interference of their chief to quiet them, and restore harmony. The tree being thus sawed down, it was then trimmed of all its limbs, and the top cut off where, after all the bark and sap should be shaved off, it would leave the heart part of the diameter of about one and a quarter inches. All the limbs were trimmed out in this manner, and the gang continued working on the mountain, sawing down, and trimming out until a sufficient load for the whole gang to carry down to the landing was obtained. Several days were spent at work in the mountain woods at each excursion, before a full load of body and limbs for all the gang, was prepared ; they then collected it all at one spot, the chief set off the load for each one, or for three, or five, or more as required ; they then shouldered it, and all in Indian file proceeded down the mountain with their burdens to the landing place. The ship's men under the directions of the carpenter, and his mates, with some natives to assist, saw and cut the body and limbs to proper lengths of between four and five feet, and then shave off, with the drawing knife, all the bark and sap. It is then in merchantable order for shipping on board, and the king is paid for the lot, as has been previously agreed. He then sends it off alongside the ship, and immediately divides the purchased articles with the chief, who has with his gang performed the task with his men in procuring the wood.

September 6th.—Having completed our business here, and the Hope having now a full cargo on board, we unmoored ship, took up our anchors, bore away, and steered for a leeward passage through the outer sea wall reef. We were surrounded by masses of natives of both sexes making the air ring with their friendly parting shouts; but above all, was the parting between His Majesty and Mr. Brown. The king had become so affectionately attached to him as his adopted son, that he took him again, and again in his arms, and by his parental hugs of embrace raised him from the deck, as if a child. When in his canoe returning for the shore, he kept up the parting signals until beyond sight from the deck; but even then he could be observed from aloft. We were now under all sail, with a fine trade breeze from E.S.E. and pleasant weather, steering across the bay, and out through the passage in the main reef by what I thought properly named Union Passage, because on one of its reefy points the ship Union was so unfortunately wrecked, and all on board of her, but the Tonga pilot perished, or were massacred by these cannibals as soon as they obtained a footing on any dry part of the outer wall reef. Precisely at noon we passed safely through Union Passage, when Sandal Wood Road bore E.N.E. distant 3 leagues, and at same time the east chop of Sandal Wood Bay, which I named Sandy Hook Point (which it so much resembles) bore east, distant four miles. We were now engaged in clearing up the decks, lashing water casks, &c., in sea preparation.

September 7th.—At 3, P. M., Levo Callow Island was in sight bearing W.N.W. distant 7 leagues, and now a fresh trade wind and a heavy rolling sea accompanied us. This made it necessary to reduce the ship's canvass to her double-reefed topsails. At 8, P. M., I thought it prudent to bring the ship to the wind, and to spend the night on short tacks, keeping her throughout the night as near the spot we now were as possible. At 6, A. M., bore away and made sail, when immediately after, the officer on the look out station aloft, gave the alarm call, that our ship was over discoloured water, and on casting my eye over the rail I could plainly see the bottom composed of coral rocks, to appearance about four fathoms of water: I instantly ordered the ship to be brought to the wind to make a board off to a clear sea again, when in a few minutes, in short, before the ship's sails were fairly trimmed to the wind, we were out of danger or had lost sight of the bottom, and to appearance, were again off soundings. When the ship was on the shoal Levo Callow bore W.N.W. distant 6 leagues, and the centre of Antua Island, E.½N. distant 8 leagues. At noon Levo Callow bore E. by S.½ S. distant 3 leagues, at which time the ship's latitude was 16° 41′ S.

September 8th.—At 2, P. M., Levo Callow bore S.E. by E. distant 7 leagues. At sun setting, strong gale, with cloudy thick weather. I thought it again prudent to haul the ship on the wind, and to spend the night under close-reefed topsails, with the endeavour during it, to keep her as near her present station as possible. At 6, A. M., bore away and made all sail on our course for Canton in China. Variation at this time 12° 9′ east.

September 17th.—At 4, P. M., the look-out aloft gave out the sound of "Land, ho!" which proved to be two high islands lying east and west of each other. One bore N. by E. and the other N. by E.½E. distant 7 leagues. Our latitude at this time was 12° 25′ south, and at the north-westward of the westernmost of those two islands, we observed a small island or islet, in its appearance very much like the Eddy Stone off Van Diemen's Land. These being wide to the windward of our course, and night closing in upon us, we have nothing farther to remark relative to them; and as it is somewhat doubtful, as to their being a new discovery I did not give them a name.

September 26*th.* — Our situation this day brings us near to the brink of crossing the equator the second time, out of the four crossings we shall have to make during our voyage. The weather ever since our departure from the Feejee Archipelago has been so cloudy and thick as to prevent our lunar sights until this day, when by two sets of very good observations, the mean of them gave the ship's longitude to be 163° 42′ 20″ east, and her latitude 1° 33′ south, and variation 10° east, our longitude by celestial observations differing about four degrees from our longitude by account in this short run from the Feejees. This shows that we must, and very recently, I judge, have had an unaccountably strong current* to have set

* Subsequently in the ship Cadmus, bound for Calcutta, on crossing the equator in about the eighty-eighth degree of east longitude, in the Indian Ocean, I met with, and experienced the like currents. R. B.

our ship so wide from my intended route, which was to have kept in the track of the Walpool, Captain Butler. He appeared by his account to have made a very clear passage, but by the effect of the current, we now found our ship on an entirely new route.

Here the author would respectfully ask: what is the cause of those never-ceasing, or frequent, rapid, unaccountable, and variable currents, in all parts, or places near the equator on our globe, as they appear to be the same in the Pacific, in the Indian Ocean, and in the South Atlantic, between the continents of America and Africa? Are they caused by the force of the heavy gales in the variable latitudes on the surface of Neptune's element? or by the daily rotation of our globe, as some will have it, and the trade winds? It cannot, I think, be the last; for if so, they would be regular, and always setting the same way, and not suddenly variable. It seems, therefore, all we can say relative to the explanation of the fact, is, that it is one of those mysteries known only to that Almighty Being, who created our globe, and placed it in its orbit.

October 3d, 1807.—At 6, A. M., the look-out at masthead, surprised us by "Land, ho!" bearing N.W. by W. to W. by N. which at first had the appearance of two islands; but on nearing it, we plainly discovered the two elevations to be joined by low land. At noon the centre of the land bore west ¼ N. distant 5 leagues, and I place it in latitude 5° 15′ north, and longitude 165° 17′ east of London. It not appearing on any chart, or in any book in my possession I consider it a new discovery, and have named it, Hope's Island.

Sunday, October 25th.—We were in sight of the Phillipine Islands, Say-pan, Tinian and Agrigan; but after so long an absence from our much-beloved country, and being very anxious to meet with our friends whom we expected to find in Canton, we did not stop to obtain and partake of the many excellent articles said to be procured at those beautifully green looking islands. Having a fresh and fair trade wind we passed them, with mouths watering, and proceeded on, with all despatch.—I place Anson's Road in Tinian, in latitude 15° 01′ north, longitude 145° 47′ east.

November 9th, 1807.—We had sight of Tobago-Sima, and soon after, the high-peaked mountain on Formosa. In a short time we passed the Vela Retta rocks, south of them at three miles distance. At 6, P. M., the south end of Formosa bore N.N.E., distant 9 leagues.

November 12th.—On this day we obtained sight of the land, and islands off the coast of

China, passed several fleet of fishing craft, and on arriving among the islands we obtained a pilot for Macoa. After touching there, we proceeded up the river to Whampoa, where we had the gratification of meeting our friends, and receiving our letters, and news from home. After exchanging our cargo we received on board a cargo of teas and other China goods.

December 27th.—We sailed from Whampoa for home, "sweet home."—Nothing unusual occurred during our passage, and we arrived safe at New-York on the 3d of May, 1808, with, it is believed, a perfectly satisfactory voyage to all concerned.—We now learned that a stern, and rigid embargo was in force throughout the United States.

CHAPTER VIII.

A list of the native names of sixty-four of the principal islands of the Archipelago of the Feejee group, with remarks.

Fatoa, (*Turtle*)
Honghare Lili,
Honghare Levo,
Folongaa,
Henghare,
Annamooka,
Henghasaw Levo,
Mertta,
Allakippa,
Iaa,
Iaa Livi,
Uheda,
Body,
Nahow,
Gorroo,
Waanewawattee,

Marraboo,
Cabbarria,
Voangabba,
Ollarwa, (saddle)
Como,
Cannaetah,
Wattaharre-nahow,
Kyerratta,
Gerroa,
Freenoo,
Dudua,
Foona,
Toconroba,
Vakkia,
Gorra,
Niroa,
Bakiky,
Woohiah,
Nyengany,
Vohia,
Ohohia, Lili,
Mahhini,
Ohokia,
Bollowhu,
Mackini,
Onratta,
Chucheeah,
Dabuctah,
Wattaharra,
Dedea,
Omango,
Nyri,
Volkkia,
Ohohia Lavo,
Onhow,
Battika,
Gorrobou,
Batallie,
Volahue,
Booyee,
Levo-Callow,
Antua,
Assavo,
Ambow,
Hongasaw,
Direction-Island, (by us so named)
Honghary,
Furia. (This is a very high, mountainous island, and I presume has been a volcano.)

REMARKS.—There is also in this group a number of small islands, and islets, the native names of which were not obtained, and of course are not noticed in this list.

PART II.

SKETCH DESCRIPTIVE OF THE WHALE CHASE, SHOWING THE DANGER, AND DARING BRAVERY OF THE OFFICERS AND SEAMEN IN ATTACKING AND CONQUERING THESE MONSTERS OF THE DEEP, TOGETHER WITH THE PROCESS OF CUTTING IN, &c., &c.

CHAPTER I.

Whale chase—Danger in fastening to—Condition of the whale—Whalers' preference to full grown—These most troublesome—Sounding of the whale—The signal—Breakwater roar of the monster—Terrific scene—Snowy foam of the sea—Fatal stroke—Sea of blood—His dying flurry—Life extinct—Huge inanimate mass on the surface of the sea—Lamentable end of poor Bob—His character.

THE ship being on the whaling ground in the right season, and when on the earnest hunting chase in those beautiful alert craft, the whale boats, the danger in fastening, and killing a whale is by no means at all times equal. On some occasions they are killed without hardly an effort, or struggle, at others two or three hours elapse before this can be effected, owing mostly to the nature of the whale's condition, whether plump and thriving, or lank and lean, and also partly to the chance of fastening.—

Whalers most generally prefer fastening to a full grown, or old whale, if a well fed one, as he is less inclined to give battle than a younger one. A right, or black whale, that will yield about forty barrels of oil is in general the most troublesome. When fastened to by the thrust of the iron (harpoon) to which the line is fast, he, (if in deep water) immediately sounds, taking out of the boat from sixty to eighty fathoms, or more of line. At these depths he remains until want of air forces him to the surface again, which usually will be about thirty minutes. Care must be now taken to prevent him from coming up under and staving the boat. The line as he rises is hauled in, and carefully coiled in the stern sheets of the boat, the men (in vulgar phrase) being wide awake, ready at their oars for the least signal. When the rushing sound of the water, accompanied by the roar of the monster announce his arrival to the surface, the word is given by the officer to haul on. The bow-man now prepares his lance, the boat is hauled by the warp as close as possible to the whale, and the lance vigorously plied in thrusts, by darts. The whale unable as yet to sound, becomes infuriated by the repeated thrusts of the lance, and a scene commences, of which only those who have witnessed it, can have any idea. The huge monster of the deep galled and rendered mad with pain, cuts through the water with amazing velocity, now this way, now that, requiring all the skill of the officers, and exertions of the men to manage the boat so as to avoid him, and his enormous flukes (finned tail) lash the water into a snowy foam. Soon after the blood spouting from his lanced wounds, stains with blood the sea around him; and now and then a thundering roar is heard as the lance of his tormenters aggravates his pain. At last the fatal stroke and wound is given, when his life's blood is spouted on high. Seeing this, the boats are laid off from him, so as to be out of his way, when he goes into his flurry, or dying agonies. This soon comes on; his huge body is agitated; he lashes the surface of the sea, incessantly, and is surrounded with a thick, bloody foam. His efforts become gradually weaker; when, on a sudden, they cease, and the late living body lies a huge inanimate mass on the surface of the ocean. On one of those chases, and anxious slaughtering attacks, we had before our eyes, the following melancholy and painful occurrence. This was the lamentable misfortune to lose one of our crew, a harpooner, by a whale. Poor Bob! he was a first-rate, and uncommonly expert whaler; nevertheless, fate, it seems, had decreed, that his time had come,

He was truly an excellent man, at all times willing, and pleasant; beloved by all on board, and out of all the crew no one could have been taken whose loss would have been more felt. He was a first-rate seaman, as well as a courageous whaler; in short, such a valuable man as is always much wanted, and seldom found aboard ship. As such his loss was severely felt.—He was suddenly taken from out the boat overboard by the warp attached to the preventer, the harpoon fouling some part of his body, or limbs (his arm, it was supposed) while performing his duty as harpooner. In the act of darting the preventer iron, he was seen to go over board, when the line was immediately cut, in the hope of picking him up; but in vain, we never saw him more. Poor Bob! his death must have been speedy, as the whale was then sounding at a fast rate.

CHAPTER II.

Cutting in the whale—Cutting gear—Manner of cutting in—Blubber blankets—Mincing blubber—Trying out oil—Whale bone—Average quantity to a fish.

WHEN a whale is about to be cut in (or in other words,) stripped of his fat, or blubber, he is taken alongside the vessel with his head towards her stern, and the cutting gear is then prepared. This gear consists of two wind-tackle falls, the straps of the blocks being toggled through their bights to pendants from the mainmast-head. These pendants are then guyed forward so as to bring the falls directly over the main, or blubber hatch. The ends of the falls are then brought to the windlass, and three or four turns taken round it with each end, a stopper being in readiness to clap on either fall. A man now jumps upon the whale, places a strap on his fin, and the fall is attached to it. The whale is then hove by it side up, and the fall stoppered; small stages are placed outside the gunnel on which stand the officers about to cut the blubber, provided with sharp spades fastened on the shaft, eight or ten feet long. The head with the bone attached to it is now cut off and hove in, with the other fall, and placed aft on the deck. The fall is then overhauled down again, and the throat, lips, and tongue are next hove in, and lowered down the hatch between decks. The other fall is then attached to the end piece hove on, and a strip of fat with the skin, or blubber (as it is termed) from four to five feet wide is hoisted up, the officers on the stages constantly cutting with their spades on each side of the piece, or strip until the fall is hove block, and block. The stopper is now passed, the other fall overhauled down, and a slit, or hole cut in the blubber piece for a new end (or as it is called in the blanket piece) with a boarding knife. The bight of the block strap is passed through, and a toggle through it, and the fall is hove on as soon as it takes the strain. The blubber of the blanket piece of the first tackle is cut through, and off above the toggle slit, with the same large knife. The blubber piece, or blanket thus cut off is lowered down the hatch into the blubber room; and so on, one fall relieving the other, rolling the fish over and hoisting in the blubber, until all is stripped off. The blubber blankets are then cut up into small pieces, taken to the large table, and the lean attached to the fat flinched off. They are then minced, and thus made ready for the try pots. The try pots are started in the trying by pouring about a barrel of oil, into each pot, or kettle, and then kindling a fire in the furnace beneath. When this oil is sufficiently heated, the minced blubber is thrown in, and in about the space of half an hour it will be sufficiently boiled. It is then baled off with the ladle, leaving 40 to 50 gallons in each pot, (these pots hold from 150 to 180 gallons.) The scraps are taken out with a skimmer into a scrap tub, and the kettles are then ready for a fresh supply, which is immediately thrown in. After the kettles are heated by the first turn, the oil boils out much quicker. If good blubber and well tried the scraps will be chip dry, and the scraps constantly supply the work with ample fuel. With such sized kettles well attended, about fifteen barrels of oil can be boiled out of a fair lot of blubber, in a six hours' watch, making an average of say 50 barrels in 24 hours. The oil is baled from the pots into a copper cooler fitted with a strainer, from which it passes into the deck pot, and is baled from thence into the casks. The casks should be well shrunk, twice or more filled for this purpose with hot oil, until they have stopped shrinking. When well coopered, after being finally and thoroughly thus shrunk, with hot oil, they will retain the oil safe home without loss by leakage. The whale bone generally averages 800 pounds to a hundred barrels of oil, some whales over a thousand weight, others again only four or five hundred, the bone is cut out at its upper end, from the lower part of the head, eight or ten slabs at a time. Each slab, is then cut separately apart, and scraped, the gum extracted, and then stowed away below. Particular care should be taken to have the slabs dry when stowed, as otherwise they would be very likely to damage, and perhaps if stowed away not dry be entirely spoiled, or at least much damaged, during the long passage home.

The whale is an affectionate creature to its kind. It nurses its young like the cow,—and while in tender infancy, basking with its mother at the surface of their element, if an alarm affrights her, she immediately takes her young under her fin, and instantly dives to a prudent depth. When going through the water, partly on her side with her glistening round eye she looks up to the surface, as she swims along, as it appears, with the endeavour to discover the cause of the danger. If the alarm has been given by a boat, and the boat is within view, over her, she keeps her eye, as it were rivetted on it, as long as it remains within her sight. J. E. B.

CHAPTER III.

Rook of the Falklands—Its sagacious, saucy cunning—Its size and colour—Its strength and gripe of claws—Its shrewdness in watching—Its seemingly intelligent language—Mischievous thievery—A glove chase and failure—Superior knowledge of the bird.

AMONG the great variety of the feathered race at the Falkland Islands, the rook is the most sagacious and cunning. Its wise and fox-like actions are astonishing, and, without personal observation, almost beyond belief:—The rook is about the size of the grouse, of a black or dark-brown colour; its beak and legs of a light yellow; its beak is of iron strength for a nip, and the gripe of its talons are truly death-like. In all parts of those Islands, those who land from their boat, will surely, the moment that they step foot on shore, be surrounded and accompanied by a look-out flock, as sentries, canting their head one way and the other, with their scrutinizing eye, as if to pierce your very thoughts and intentions. They are, apparently, very earnest and mischievous, watching your every motion, and as you advance forward they will accompany you, hopping and flying from prominences of rock, or bog, watching your actions with an eye of piercing attention, and a sage look. They will examine, after you, every minute article or thing you may stop to observe or inspect. If you disturb a turf by turning, or perforate the surface, or make an excavation in the soil or earth, as soon as you have left it, the rook will immediately examine the spot, with eye, beak, and talons, in the most minute manner, making at same time, in their squalling language to each other, a cackling, screaming noise, with head and neck stretched up, which they appear perfectly to understand. If you happen to lay down and leave your knife, or other article, by the spot, they will promptly seize and make sure possession of it and carry it off; and except you give chase as they retreat and thereby obtain now and then a sight of it in their claws or beak, (which they will readily exhibit from time to time in the chase, and seem to delight in it, as they constantly retreat and tantalize you, keeping at a proper distance,) you may be sure this is all and the last you will ever see of it:—there is no remedy, unless you happen to have with you your gun charged to shoot the vexatious and impertinent thief instantly. One of our sportsmen had shot a number of geese on landing, and left them in the bows of the boat during our perambulation; when, on our return, to our utter astonishment, our boat was surrounded by a large company of those depredators, mostly keeping in pairs, each by his mate, eternally crying kā—kā—kā! —as if ridiculing our credulity. Nothing was left but the feathers and bones of the geese, which were strewed about in every direction. They are not only flesh-eaters, but are the greatest gormandizers and gluttons imaginable. Here I will mention one evidence among hundreds of the like, of the rook's superior sagacity:—On a fine, calm, pleasant morning, the author landed from his ship in the jolly-boat, accompanied only by the steward and apprentice-boy. On walking directly up the green bank, attended, of course, by the usual company of rooks on guard, I fell in with a patch of wild potatoes, growing spontaneously among the green grass, the tops of their vines being a few inches above it. I laid my woollen glove on the rock, taking up a bit of a stick to dig and examine the size of their roots. Although engaged not two yards from my glove, before I was aware, and as quick as thought, up ran Mr. Rook, snatched up the glove, flew a few rods with it,—then lit on a bog, laid the glove down by him, and looked back at me with an arch-like, mischievous eye;—as if intending to say, "I have out-generalled you this time; and now, get your glove again if you can!" In his exultation, he was joined by his mate, and they commenced conversation in their screams of kā,—kā,—kā! Being much vexed, with my two aids, we started on an attack, with stones, not having with me my fowling-piece. On getting within two or three rods of him, he would pick up the glove and hop, run, or fly, some five or eight rods, then rest on bog, or rock, and lay down, by his side, the glove again, and then wait, in screams of exultation, our fire of stones, hove by myself, steward, and boy. Thus fleeting on for upwards of a mile, this cunning bird fooled us, certainly in the distance, more than fifty times, until he completely tired out our force, and obliged us to give up the chase, and to leave him and his companion in possesion of their stolen prize. We had no remedy, but were forced to put up with their taunts and sarcastic eyeings towards us, seemingly much to their high gratification. Thus dishonoured by the loss of the glove and victory, we returned to our boat, and on board ship, well tired out by the unsuccessful chase.

In fact, the Falkland Rook is, unquestionably, the most knowing, mischievous, and saucy bird among the feathered race ;—and gives to the way-worn sailors much vexatious trouble, during their hunting and sealing excursions. If a knife and steel, a powder-horn, roundabout jacket, or other article, which they are able to take away in their claws, or beak, be laid down by their side, unattended but for a minute, as they are ever on the watch, it will be seized by the rook and carried off. Without the charged gun in hand, it will be very difficult ever to obtain the article again. On committing the theft they will call each other and gather around it on rock, or bog, scrutinizing it, with sageness on their visage, and their sharp, bright, piercing eye, with a sarcastic look, first at you, then on the article they have stolen, and so on as long as you are near by, wishfully desirous to re-possess your property, and, ever and anon at such times, are accompanied with their croaking screams, directed to each other:—It is truly the sapient fox, among the winged race.

PART III.

NARRATIVE SKETCH OF A VOYAGE OF THE SHIP TONQUIN, UNDER THE COMMAND OF THE AUTHOR, TO THE CHINA SEA, IN THE YEARS 1807—1808.

CHAPTER I.

Building of the ship—Great despatch in performance—Occurrence on the wild coast of Java—A terrific savage—A white boy to roast—Fright of boy Bill—Secret retreat in a bread cask—Investigation of a singular affair.

THE Tonquin, this beautifully modelled and first-rate ship, was built by those well-known ship-wrights, Messrs. Adam and Noah Brown, at their ship-yard, in New-York city, for the China trade, under the superintendence and inspection of the author. She was double-flush decked, and pierced for 22 guns, and proved a fast sailing vessel, of speed, perhaps, equal to any sloop of war of the navy. Her burthen was rather under 300 tons, and her keel was laid on the blocks on the first day of March, 1807. She was launched, and sailed from the port of New-York for China, on the 26th day of May, 1807, under the command

and direction of the author, and arrived back at the same port from her voyage to Canton, with a full cargo of China goods, March 6th, 1808. Thus she was built, coppered, rigged, launched, and performed her voyage to China and back, in the short space of 12 months and 6 days from the day her keel was laid on the blocks. —Impressed with this, I believe that it is doubtful, if there be an instance on record of such singularly unexampled skill and despatch of performance in the ship-wright business, and nautical management, of or from any country or nation existing, as in the case of this ship, on this, her construction and voyage. What transpired and occurred, other than what would be expected on a similar ordinary voyage to Canton and back, during this voyage in the Tonquin, is hereby related in the following, viz:—

A singular affair when off the wild coast of Java,—and also the transactions mentioned and met with on the passage up the China sea, and while at Canton.

On our passage out, after entering the Strait of Sunda, our ship had arrived abreast of a bay, on the Java shore, a short distance eastward of Mew Island. During the night in a calm, she was set by the current in shore, into such shoal water, that it became prudent to bring her to an anchor at a short distance, somewhat less than a mile, from the shore of this wild native coast. When morning came we found our ship situated thus, near the shore. As soon as broad day-light came, the natives, observing the ship so near, riding at anchor, an opportunity so inviting to them, came off in their canoes; but all, save one, keeping just without hailing distance. That one contained only a single native, whom we presumed to be a chief, as he was gaudily dressed, and accoutred with a feather cap, mounted on his cranium, with waving plumes stuck in or attached to it, made of the feathers plucked from that courageous monarch of the *barn-yard*, the male domestic fowl. His face was painted in streaks, or characters, with colours of red and white. Thus beautified, his jet-black teeth, contrasted with his blood-red lips;—he was truly savage! In fact, his whole appearance was wild and fantastic indeed; and while, according to their custom and habit of sitting with much native pride, thus accoutred in his canoe, which had a line fast to the ship's quarter, he was thus situated when the author came on deck.

On emerging from the companion gangway, I observed the first officer, Mr. Mackay, a very worthy nautical citizen, as well as of a very pleasant disposition, leaning over the quarter-railing, and endeavouring, by signs, &c., to barter with this singularly adorned native in the canoe, for the fowls, fruit, &c., he had brought off. Close by the officer's side, on tiptoes, to enable him to see over the rail, peeping over it, with his eyes rivetted on the savage in the canoe, was my apprentice-boy Bill, an active, quick, observing child, now only in his eighth year. On my observing to Mr. Mackay, "What have we here, and what does this barbarian want?" he answered, "a native, sir, from this wild coast; and it seems he has come off from the shore to trade—I am trying to barter with him for the refreshments he has brought off;" then dryly adding, "he appears disposed not to be willing to receive any thing for them which we can conveniently spare, but wants and insists upon a white boy to roast!"—Bill, on hearing these words, looked up at the first officer, much affrighted, and then at me, with a most pitiful countenance:—observing the boy in such affright, and to put him at his ease again, I said kindly to him, "Never you mind, Bill, what this savage-looking fellow wants; if you continue to be, as heretofore, a smart and good-behaved boy, neither he nor any other man-eating savage shall have you to roast, not if he would give us our ship full of gold,—nor for all the fowls and fruit the whole race of them on shore can produce; therefore keep your mind easy, and go to your duty with the steward." Bill made his bow, with thanks, and marched off to the steward's room. At that time, nothing more was thought or said on the subject. The barter being soon finally accomplished with the native, he paid, and the fowls, fruit, &c., received on board, a breeze springing up from off the land, the ship was immediately got under way, and the natives all left us for the shore, our ship steering out of the bay. At eight bells, the steward came to set the breakfast table, (a part of the boy Bill's duty being to keep the knives and forks scoured bright,) and now wanting the knives and forks, no Bill was to be found! On the alarm being given that he was missing, the ship was thoroughly searched fore and aft, below and aloft, but no boy Bill could be found, or any answer obtained, to the loud calls on his name. In this dilemma, painful as it was to my own feelings, and to those of the officers, particularly of Mr. Mackay, I presume there was not one on board, but now felt for the loss of poor boy Bill. Being thus painfully disappointed, after our thorough search throughout every part of the ship, we were forced to come to the conclusion, that the boy, in or during the usual bustle of weighing anchor, had, unobserved, got knocked, or fallen overboard, and was drowned. This sad conclusion of ours was then fully believed by us all; and it was heart-rending to myself and officers, thus to lose our sprightly boy.

In this belief we remained until the afternoon of the third day, when, to our very agreeable surprise, the enigma was explained, by the boy Bill appearing in full life before our view! and all were relieved from distressful feelings, because Bill was alive and among us again.

On investigating this very remarkable and singular affair, it appeared, that, after making the land, (Java Head,) on the day previous to anchoring, in the evening after passing the Head, and entering the strait, the seamen in their circle on the forecastle, had been relating their tough-yarns, relative to the kind of people which inhabited this land, to which the ship was now so near. Such an extensive country of mountains and valleys, covered by a wilderness of forest trees, in such green, and luxurious appearance must have numerous inhabitants of some kind of people; and some two or three of their number that had passed along here before, declared that they were savages of the worst kind, and known to be man-eaters. Nothing could please them so well, as they had been informed, as to have a fat, well-fed white person, to roast, or bake in the ground, after their manner of cooking, to make a good meal, in their gormandizing cannibal feasts. To this tough-yarn, the boy Bill (unknown to the author until subsequently after the embezzlement of himself) had been an attentive listener. And when he placed himself in the morning by the side of the first officer, to have a view of the savage in his canoe, he had asked what that ugly looking fellow wanted. Mr. Mackay jocosely answered him, "the fellow, Bill, is endeavouring to make me understand, that he wants a white boy to roast." Just at this moment the author stepped up to join them from the cabin gang-way, as before related, and addressed to Mr. M. his inquiry: Bill was then sent away to the steward's room. Knowing that the steward some few days previous, in replenishing his bread room, had taken a moiety of the bread out of a large bread cask, and headed up the cask again, a side piece of the heading which had got broken, having been flung aside, and not put again in its place, in the heading of it up, Bill remembered, that in this condition the cask had been stowed back in its berth again among its fellows, in the ship's waist below deck, and had left a breakage of a few inches between its deficient broken head, and the next cask, in the longer, or tier forward of it, just sufficient for him to squeeze his body through, and into the nulledge bread cask. On the steward's leaving him in his room, the morning he was missing, to go on deck at the time the ship was getting under way, Bill as he subsequently confessed, did not feel perfectly safe, or surely certain (his own words) but that the ugly looking savage, might yet persuade us to deliver him up or succeed in getting him to roast. It made him, he said, feel dreadfully horrible, (still all his own words) notwithstanding what the author had said to encourage, to cheer up, and also assured him he had nothing to fear, had not the intended effect, as the trouble on his mind. All this induced him, nevertheless, on thinking of the bread cask to promptly repair to it, and stow himself in, while the steward was on deck. He went therefore and crept into the nulledge cask, and did not answer when called to, as he feared the ugly savage would not be gone. Here secreted he had subsisted on the bread, cautiously coming out in the dead, or still time of the night to the steward's pitcher for a drink of water, and quickly back again to his hiding place. Thus sly, he had remained undiscovered until this afternoon, being the third day of his being missing; when the steward on proceeding with the cooper and his gang, to recruit again his store of bread in the bread room, on parbuckling out, and unheading this nulledge cask, behold, there was discovered, sitting with his chin on his knees, monkey like, our lost, supposed drowned, and missing boy Bill, who pertly looked up as if nothing unusual had occurred, as if nothing had taken place out of the ordinary and daily course of affairs. He quickly asked the steward, before moving to get out, if that ugly Indian was gone.

CHAPTER II.

Ship arrives at Macoa—A speck of war—A typhoon—British squadron—Poolo Sapata and Baltimore Company ship—Raging sea—Singular effect of—Change of the monsoon—Passage up the Tygris—Commodore Pelew—His declaration—State of war—President and U. S. consul—Unpleasant state of affairs—Author's determination to put to sea—Chinese pilot, and boat—The agreement.

On our ship's arrival at Macoa, we found the state of affairs rather war-like, between our countrymen, the Americans, and English; which, it was said, had been caused by an attempt, by the order of the commander of a

British brig of war, to press the men out of an armed American Baltimore schooner. This brought on a battle between them, in which the captain of the schooner was reported to have been slain, as also a lieutenant of the brig, with some few men on both sides. The schooner was carried, and taken by boarding, and sent to Calcutta. This the author found to be the situation of affairs on anchoring in the road at Macoa.

On referring back I would here remark, that on our passage across and up the China sea, we experienced one of those violent Typhoons, to which this sea is subject, in which at some degrees to the north-east of our situation at the time of its greatest violence, and nearer to the China coast than our ship then was, were a British squadron consisting of two frigates, and a sloop of war; also, in their company were two East India ships, with an American ship belonging to Boston, which were, by the information we subsequently received, all dismasted in this Typhoon. The smaller 36 gun frigate, it was said, worked much in her frame, by the effect of the storm and sea, and the weight of her metal, she having at one time, as report stated, ten feet water in her hold, and was forced to throw overboard, as a sacrifice to Neptune, monarch of the ocean, for their safety, and as a contribution to His Majesty's element, the greatest part of her guns, to enable them to free her, prevent her from foundering, and survive the Typhoon; with regard to ourselves on passing the Island of Poloo Sapata, and entering the China sea, we had then the commencement of this gale and violent storm from the west-south-west, at which time, while our ship was scudding on her course under a reefed foresail, we passed under the stern of the Baltimore China Company's ship, which was at the time lying to under her storm sails, and which did not, by such plan of procedure or judgment, arrive in Canton until forty-three days after our ship. This gale having increased into the Typhoon, and thereby changed the monsoon in the China sea, and settled it, in the opposite one, blew from the north-east quarter of the compass, in a steady wind, of course, in seaman's phrase, dead-a-head, or, after the gale and Typhoon were over, directly against the Baltimore ship's course which was to pass up across the China sea. On the contrary, by our improving it, and scudding before this fair gale, we run our ship across the Macklesfield Bank, and thus secured our passage. During the heaviest part of the Typhoon, we were crossing over the northern part of the Macklesfield Bank, and at this time our good little ship was ploughing the surface of the foaming and raging sea, as buoyantly and as lively as a duck. The Typhoon was now blowing from the point of compass S.S.W. and driving us along at the rate of ten or eleven miles per hour. Our top-gallant-yards were on deck, the masts housed, all steering-sail booms down on deck from off the yards, and every sail was furled, and double stopped, or bound to the yards with double gasketing, and additional lines. Every thing was as snug as our skill and rope lashings could make them, and not a yard or stitch of canvass was set. Thus snug, and thus swiftly were we gliding along over the foaming surface, and as it were flying before the raging elements; yet we nevertheless experienced while going at this rate during the space of about fourteen hours, the following extraordinary fact, which I had never before observed. This was the uncommon force and singular effect of the motion of the raging seas, which would break against our alert ship's stern in such a manner, with such violent rage, and with such giant-like force, as to sweep over her tafferel and roll forward on the deck over and over, as on a beach. Generally each foaming sea broke at the author's station by the wheels-man. Secured by rope to assist the cun, two resolute, cool, and thorough bred tars, were at the wheel. Here it was about middle-waist deep, as it broke over the tafferel and rolled forward. These strokes of white wave force were so great, and of such weight when they broke against the ship's stern, that they dashed the yawl boat, in her tackles against the stern, so as to bring the boat's gunwales so near together, as to be but half their correct distance apart, driving the ends of her thawts, or plank seats through her sides. When our ship thus received these strokes of the sea or wave, she would tremble, in common saying, like an aspen leaf, in the wind, but still like a good race horse of sterling bottom would keep alert on her legs; as a sportsman would say.

The Cun.—To the helmsman,—Steady,—steady, sir,—port,—port, sir,—steady,—steady, sir,—starboard—starboard, sir,—port steady,—steady, sir,—that's well-done, my good fellows,—and keep a sharp eye at the swing of her bows,—ay-ay, sir, starboard hard a-starboard,—hard a-starboard, sir,—port steady,—steady, sir,—that's handsome, my lads, cheerly, cheerly, our good bark glides over the mountain wave like a duck, be careful to keep your quids,* my brave fellows, like true tars, on the

* Jack Tar's mouthful of negro head tobacco, not over the size of a hen's egg.

right side, and she will carry us safe, rely on it. When the Typhoon ceased, the wind during it, having gradually veered around to the south-south-east, and to east, it fell calm, for a few hours, leaving with us an ugly cross sea, in which our ship was now compelled to labour, and making it very uncomfortable for us on board, she wallowing, rolling, and jerking, as if to strain every bolt, and yarn out of its place. However, we had now the satisfaction to comfort us, that during the violent Typhoon, we had escaped from all damage of note, saved our masts and spars, and had the good fortune to run our ship up the China sea, to a station in the north-east part of it. This secured our prompt passage to Canton, against the north-east monsoon, when it should set in ; which it soon did, as we had conjectured. It set in with a regular monsoon breeze springing up from the north-east, when we made sail and steered in for the China coast; as our ship passed along, we had a view of the Island of Pedro Banca. After passing it, and on arriving near the Lema Islands, we obtained a pilot for Macoa, who brought the ship at anchor in the road abreast of that city. Early the next morning, the author, by the aid of his boat, paid a visit to that city for the purpose of procuring (according to the China custom) a river pilot for the ship to Whampoa, and a Mandarin pass for Canton, which for every ship or vessel bound up the river must be here first procured. As soon as these were accomplished, the author returned on board, and the Chinese pilot shortly after came off on board, when our ship was immediately got under way, moving on her passage up the river Tygris.

On passing the British squadron consisting at this time of two frigates, a sloop, and brig of war at anchor at Lin-ting, a boat with a lieutenant, and a petty officer came alongside our ship and the officers stepped promptly on board. In the instant after the shake of the hand, the lieutenant, cast an eye aloft, then fore and aft, and turning to the author with a look of much surprise in his countenance, said: "Had you not the Typhoon?" "Yes, sir, in its highest rage, I believe." "How the d—l then did you contrive to save your masts,—our ships were all dismasted, and we had our hands fully employed to keep them above water,—there is also a countryman of yours here, a Bostonian, that was dismasted in it, who is now at anchor at an island below; but, by the lion, I cannot see about your ship a yarn stranded, or spar injured. Why, my good sir, your ship appears as if just out of your home port." We had in the short space of good weather since the Typhoon, painted and slicked up our ship to enter port to the credit of America, and now she was all-a taunto, with sky-sail yards aloft. "Thank you, sir, for your compliment; we scud our ship throughout the Typhoon, she behaved like a good boat, and did our duty in the best manner, to prevent her being wounded." "Well, sir, you will not be offended; but I must remark, Yankees, as you are, your ship gives us a rare evidence of American seamanship." After attending to the examination of our men, and finding them all Americans, they very politely wished us a safe passage up the river, and took their departure. Our ship now proceeded up through the Bocca, and passed the forts, at this place located at the chops, and on an island at the river's mouth. We kept on, steering up the river to the anchorage at Whampoa Island, which is about ten miles from the city of Canton.

Not long after our arrival here, an occurrence took place, which produced much unpleasant and acrimonious feeling between the English and Americans. It was reported to have arisen on account of some observations relating to the capture of the Baltimore schooner heretofore mentioned, which Commodore Pelew had heard of; and which, as it was told him, and as it was asserted by the Americans, supported by their consul at Canton, was much against British honour. Commodore Pelew, the eldest son of Admiral Lord Exmouth, the senior officer in command of the British fleet of men of war on this station, induced by this, intended, as was said, to make war on the Americans. In corroboration, he sent word up to Canton, that he would soon come up to Whampoa, with the boats of his fleet, and capture every American vessel there. On learning this the Americans at that anchorage, being eleven sail, mustered their forces, supercargoes, captains, officers, and men of their fleet, at a collected meeting, to decide what was best to be done. Not feeling inclined by any threat to tamely submit, it was resolved, and agreed to by all to stand by, support and defend each other to the last, and to use every honourable endeavour and means, to protect their persons and property, come what might of the threat (if true) sent up by the commodore. They determined to defend their ships with the sternest courage, and with true Yankee spirit to the last.

On this resolve every thing was promptly and properly organized. A first and second commodore to the American fleet, were named and authorized by vote, with all other necessary officers, and instantly commenced training and disciplining the whole force of the American ships' crews.

Two of the ships were selected and agreed upon as first and second commodore to the fleet, which two were dropped down, and moored in channel-way, half-a-mile below the others. A full complement of men, with additional battery train; ample ammunition, small arms, &c., were taken from the other ships, and put on board of those of the commodores. Likewise the officers and crews of all the ships were organized into divisions, and regular day and night sentries set, and relieved. Armed boats rowed guard around and through the fleet, following each other in the lapse of short spaces of time, during the night. In fact, every means were put in requisition to give the foe a warm and American reception, should he come up and attack them, and to thus defend and retain possession of our ships and property, as well as our persons, at every risk. Thus it was a complete state of war. In this condition were affairs situated, when the author's ship, the Tonquin, had received all her cargo on board, and was ready for sea. Two other American ships had also been ready for sea for some days previous, but their captains and supercargoes did not think it proper to risk sailing, under the belief that they would surely be captured by commodore Pelew's squadron, and sent to Calcutta, agreeably to his reported threat; they therefore remained still at Whampoa, in indecision.

As soon as it was promulgated that the Tonquin would immediately sail, and run the risk, all eyes, as it were, were directed to this ship. However, the author, while in the state of war, as related, had seen commodore Pelew, up at Canton, who was then informed by the president of the British East India Company's Council, that the author was the same person to whom the commodore's father, Lord Exmouth, had showed such friendly favour, some years previous at Falmouth, in England, when the now commodore was a middy on board his father's frigate. By this occurrence, he now recognised the author, and it brought fresh to his recollection his father's friendly notice, at that previous time, to him. The author was now advised of this, through his friend the president, who, with the most honourable feelings, was very anxious to have all these unpleasant difficulties removed and settled and harmony restored. The author was also most earnestly desirous to effect the same, and thereby to proceed on his passage for New-York. The United States' consul and the president, had already tried every expedient to obtain an amicable settlement of those war-like and disagreeable proceedings now on the carpet; but they had given up all present hopes of soon settling these most unpleasant difficulties. In this discouraging and hopeless situation,—and thus perplexed and unpleasantly situated, the author at once determined to lay open his mind to the president, advise with him, and then depart with his ship down the river, and make the trial to put to sea for New-York.

Accordingly, he waited on Mr. Roberts, the president, when an understanding and arrangement was concluded upon, which was:—That the author should sail with his ship down the river for sea, and should she be stopped and detained, by the men-of-war, at Ling-ting, (commodore Pelew being now at Canton city,) the author should then despatch a line to the president, stating the fact, when he would immediately, on receipt of it, wait on commodore Pelew, and try what could be done, as possibly it might open a friendly door to the amicable settlement of all difficulties, and re-establish peace and harmony.

Matters being thus arranged, the author promptly repaired on board of his ship, where he made a confidential agreement with the

Chinese pilot, to the following effect—the conditions of which were;—that if the Tonquin should be stopped and detained, by the British squadron, at anchor below the Bocca, (mouth of the river,) at Lin-ting, he, the pilot, should then send his partner, or go himself, very chop-chop, (with great despatch,) in his pilot-boat back, up the river to Canton, with the author's chop, (letter,) to any gentleman, and which should be delivered as directed, truly, very chop-chop. For this and the boat's service, and prompt delivery of the chop, the gentleman who would receive it, or the author, would pay him well, as agreed;—And if the chop did not cause his ship to be released, then the pilot should be immediately, on the return of his boat from the city to the ship, paid and dismissed.

To these conditions the pilot readily assented, and agreed also to keep his boat, with his partner in her, constantly within convenient signal distance of the Tonquin, during her passage down the river, until she should be past the British squadron, or taken and detained by them. Thus, every thing being settled and arranged, our ship was prepared and put in readiness for sea.

CHAPTER III.

Tonquin sails from Whampoa—British fleet—Ship taken by superior force—Despatch the pilot boat—Council signal displayed from the flag ship—Release of the Tonquin—Handsome and courteous conduct of the British lieutenant—Honourable and generous proceedings of Commodore Pelew, a son worthy of his noble sire, Lord Exmouth—War state ended in peace—ship departs from Grand Ladrone—Her arrival safe at New-York.

November 18*th*, 1807.—All being now on board and ready, the Tonquin was forthwith unmoored and got under way, and proceeded down the river. When near the second bar we met and boarded the Ship Hope, Captain Reuben Brumley, belonging to the same owners, Messrs. E. & H. Fanning, and W. Coles, merchants in the city of New-York. The Hope was from the Feejee Islands,* in the South Pacific, with a cargo of sandal wood, &c. The author paid a visit on board of her and after exchanging the news, friendly salutations, &c., with Captain B., bid them a good-bye, returning on board the Tonquin. At sun-setting, when within a mile of the Bocca, and fairly in

* See Voyage of the Ship Hope.

sight of the British men of war, the tide then coming in a-head, and it falling calm, the pilot anchored the ship, to wait for the morning fair tide again. At dawn of day, the tide being now again in our favour, with also a moderate, fair breeze, which had sprung up from the northward, we weighed anchor, and passing the Bocca, steered directly for the British squadron, under only our gib and staysails, being, during the time, employed in catting, and stowing our anchor, clearing up the decks in readiness for making sail, should we be permitted to pass. When within half a mile of the flag ship, a gun was fired from her, and their colours hoisted, when we displayed the American stripes and stars, at our mizen peak. On this two launches and five barges full of armed men put off from the vessels of the fleet, taking a position directly across the path of our ship's course, and as she came up with them the launches pulled a little farther off, to board us on the outer or starboard side of our ship. The barges on the inner or larboard side, pulled promptly without hailing alongside, instantly boarded, and at once filled our little ship's decks with marines and seamen led by their officers, armed and equipped ready for battle. The commanding lieutenant was received at the gangway by our first officer, Mr.

Mackay and attended aft to the quarter deck, where the author was standing by the helmsman at the wheel. Mr. Mackay observed to him, "the Captain, sir." The lieutenant then addressed the author in a commanding tone, "Sir, you will direct your helmsman to starboard his helm, luff your ship around too and bring her at anchor under our commodore's stern." "Sir, I must decline your request, as I cannot consent to give any such order, as my ship is bound direct for New-York."—"Then, sir, I shall take the liberty to do it for you," and calling to one of his seamen, "Bob, here, take the wheel." I then observed, "If you, sir, think proper so to do, it is at your peril, as I must then surrender the ship at your risk, from this time henceforth. As it would be perfect madness, and absurdity, for me now to make resistance, even in, and by the snap of a pistol, as you have to appearance landed upwards of two hundred armed men on my decks,—a little ship with twenty-four men in all, and only eight small carriage guns, it would be the height of folly to resist,—particularly when in addition the whole weight of metal of your squadron is now levelled against us. (At this time we were passing the flag ship within pistol shot distance, and all the vessels of the fleet, with their tompions out kept slewing their pieces, as we passed, and their battery pointed at us.) It certainly, therefore, would be madness in me, sir, to make the least resistance, even to the flash of a pistol." He took the irony of my remarks, and coloured, evidently much mortified at them. Altering his tone, he said, "Sir, I am sensible it is an unpleasant errand; but, I must do my duty." He then ordered my man to leave the wheel, and directed his Bob to take it, and luff the ship around under the stern of their commodore, where they brought her to an anchor, and furled her sails. The officers and men (except two officers and ten men, seamen and marines, as a possession guard,) were then ordered to repair to their boats, taking away likewise all our men with their luggage, and clothing, except myself, the first officer, steward, and an apprentice boy. The lieutenant's being the last boat, after giving the officer, that was left in charge, his orders, he stepped into it, having in her with him our second officer, and carpenter. I observed to him, that the Tonquin was now surrendered, and at his risk, taken by His Brittanic Majesty's force under, I presumed, his immediate command, and now thereby lay at his risk. To this he only bowed assent; I had previously directed Mr. Mackay, that if the British squadron should take our ship, and any of our men out of her immediately to haul down our American ensign. This he effected as the commanding lieutenant stepped into his boat, whereupon he promptly inquired of our second officer, "What are your colours now hauled down for?" "I presume that the captain has directed it, as an evidence of the surrender of our ship to you, sir." "I believe," replied the lieutenant, "your commander is a shrewd Yankee." "He is a good father to us," remarked our carpenter, "and we think we have sufficient evidence, and feel confident that he understands his duty." "He is a very singular, fatherly captain, indeed, to be sure," observed the lieutenant.

The author now caused the signal to be made for the pilot's boat, to come alongside, and gave to him my letter, or chop as he would call it, to the president. At 8, A. M., he left the ship, saying by sunset he would deliver it as directed,—and truly the sequel will prove that he did,—for at 11, A. M., on the next day Commodore Pelew's barge hove in sight, with her colours flying, coming at a rapid rate, under canvass and oars, from the city. Immediately after she got alongside the flag-ship, a signal was displayed from her main-mast, which the officer in charge of our ship, said was to call all the captains, or senior officers of the squadron to a council. This subsequently proved to be the fact. A boat was soon seen to put off from each ship and proceed alongside the commodore. In about thirty minutes thereafter our crew were seen tossing their duds and luggage into the launch, and embarking in her, when she put off, steering for the Tonquin, accompanied in advance by the barge. In this, as she came alongside of us, appeared the lieutenant, who had commanded the force which boarded and took possession of our ship, with two other officers. On their landing on our deck, he came promptly aft, and in a pleasant and polite manner bade the author a good morning. As soon as he had received the return salutation, he very courteously and mildly observed, "I have orders, sir, from Commodore Pelew, to return every individual of your crew on board of your ship again, and to take out our officers and men; and immediately to get your ship under way, and see her placed safe in the channel, to your mind, as was her position, when we boarded her. I have also farther commands from Commodore Pelew, to tender his apology for your detention, and his good wishes, that you may have a pleasant and safe passage. In addition, to ask if there is any thing that can by him be effected, for your aid, within the compass of his duty, or desire, and consistent with His Majesty's service." All this was delivered in the most pleasant, courteous, gentlemanly, and officer-like manner. In answer, the author remarked, that although he considered the act of detention of the Tonquin wrong, and injurious, he nevertheless was very thankful to Commodore Pelew, for his frank and prompt correction of the act, as well as for his kind assistance in the offer of replacing his ship in the channel again, and farther for his very friendly expressions. Being so politely and with so much friendly feeling requested, I added: "You will, my dear sir, much oblige me in communicating to Commodore Pelew, that he would place me ever under the greatest obligations, by causing peace and harmony to be again restored and established between his and my countrymen. If he will please to have this effected,—and let all the American ships pass unmolested out of the river on their passage home, it would confer on me a favour, that would be ever thankfully appreciated, gratefully remembered and acknowledged." "I certainly will deliver to the commodore your request and desire, sir; and for myself I am free to remark that I sincerely hope our unpleasant affair, in the detention of your ship, may eventually be the means of opening the door to the re-establishment of peace, and harmony; the best of good, national feelings ought ever to exist, and be cherished by us." The Tonquin's anchor was now promptly weighed, the ship bore off into the channel, and all sail was set to a light, but fair breeze. She was then luffed to, and the lieutenant with his two brother officers, after a parting glass, to our respective countries, took their leave expressing the kindest friendly wishes, for our safe arrival to our country and friends. It was subsequently ascertained that the author's wish and hope for peace turned out in the affirmative, and proved true as was desired. A friendly understanding was very soon thereafter brought about; peace and harmony were re-established; and every American ship was permitted thereafter to pass unmolested the squadron of men of war, when going in, or bound out on their passage home. Thus ended this war-like affair, by the concluding, generous and meritorious conduct of Commodore Pelew, a son every way worthy of perpetuating the honourable and creditable acts of his noble father, Lord Exmouth.

We now proceeded down the bay, passed in sight of the city of Macoa, at which time when abreast of it, we discharged our Chinese pilot, paid, and well satisfied, who very much chin-chinned us on his departure.

At 6, P. M., we took our departure from the Grand Ladrone, and without any thing occurring during our passage, more than ordinary on similar passages, we arrived safely at New-York.

PART IV.

NARRATIVE SKETCH OF THE VOYAGE OF SHIP TONQUIN TO THE SOUTH PACIFIC OCEAN, FEEJEE ISLANDS, AND ON A NEW ROUTE TO CHINA, WHEREBY IMPORTANT DISCOVERIES WERE MADE, UNDER THE COMMAND OF THAT ABLE VOYAGER, CAPTAIN R. BRUMLEY, AND THE DIRECTIVE AGENCY OF THE AUTHOR, IN THE YEARS, 1808—1809.

CHAPTER I.

The cause and object of the voyage—Embargo in the United States—President Madison—Permission to sail on, and perform the voyage—Honourable Albert Gallatin—Tonquin sails from New-York—Gough's Island—Coast of New Holland—Mount Gardner—Ship anchors in King George III. Sound—The sick with sea-scurvy landed—Natives of this part of New Holland—Departure from King George III. Sound—Remarks relative to the Sound, and anchorage—Arrival at Tongataboo—Van Diemen's Road—Barter-trade with the natives—Dangerous navigation of the Feejee Archipelago—Arrival at the Feejees—Ship visited by two young Princes—Fleet of war-canoes—Ship receives a welcome visit from King Tynahoa—The King's affectionate meeting with Mr. Brown—Ship arrives in Sandal Wood Road—Chiefs bring the cargo to the ship—Other vessels arrive, waiting removal of Taboo to trade—Tonquin has her cargo on board—Taboo raised—A truly affectionate parting with the King and young Princes.

Captain Brumley had, in his former voyage,* contracted with the King of the Feejee Islands, for a cargo of sandal wood, to be brought from the mountains, cut into its proper length, the sap shaved off and piled on the small island at the harbour of Sandal Wood Bay, ready for a ship which would be sent out after it, within the course of eighteen moons, (months,) but the now prevailing embargo in the United States prevented any ship sailing for it, unless special permission, as was provided for in the embargo law by Congress, relative to certain cases, was granted by the President of the United States. Fearing that the wood, which is highly impregnated with essential oil, would lose all its virtue and value, by evaporation, and also that the time in the contract with the King would pass, and thereby release him from the contract, to our loss of the cargo, it was concluded to apply to President Madison, state our case plainly, and lay our contract, and our novel situation before him. The case had this bearing, likewise, that if a ship was not permitted to be sent out for the cargo of sandal wood, government would lose, as well as the citizens interested, the amount of duties which would

* See Voyage of the Hope.

arise on the exchanged return-cargo of China goods.

Accordingly the owners, Messrs. E. and H. Fanning and W. Coles, merchants in the city of New-York, applied to President Madison, for permission to send out a ship Messrs. W. Coles and E. Fanning repaired to Washington city, laid the case before the Hon. Albert Gallatin, secretary of the treasury, who, after attentively hearing their explanations of its merits, &c., and their views of the proposed voyage, for which permission was requested, then gave his own views, and laid the same, with the application, before the President. His Excellency, after due consideration, granted permission for a ship to proceed to the Feejee Islands, take the cargo of wood to Canton, and then, after exchanging it there for China goods, to return with the same direct to New-York. Permission from government being now obtained, the superior, New-York built ship Tonquin, was taken up, well armed and amply fitted, in every respect, for the voyage. She was placed under the command of the well-informed and talented Captain Reuben Brumley.

Wednesday, 15*th of June*, 1808.—The Tonquin sailed from New-York, and at 3, P. M. off Sandy Hook, Captain B., with all good feelings, parted with his friends, who had accompanied him thus far to wish him a happy and pleasant voyage. At this time, also, he discharged the pilot.

The gallant ship now filled away, under a cloud of canvass, with a fine breeze from the S. by W. At 4, P. M., they took their departure from Sandy Hook light, it then bearing W. ¼ S., 3 leagues distant. And, says the journalist, except the surface of the ocean being deserted of its usual specks of white canvass, not any thing of note, (the passage being so similar to that of the Hope and others,) occurred until Monday, August 1st., when we fell in with the Brazil coast, in latitude 7° 39′ south, and at our distance of six leagues from the land, the sea-water was much coloured. Great quantities of rock-weed was floating on its surface, and, at the same time, large shoals of whales were playing around us.

August 25th.—We had sight of Gough's Island, bearing S. by E., distant 10 leagues. This island may be seen in clear weather, I presume at least, at 20 leagues distance. At noon, it bore S S.W., distant 15 leagues, and I make its latitude to be 40° 24′ south, longitude, 10° 46′ west, variation 16° 20′ west.

Friday, 7th of October, 1808.—The coast of New Holland was in sight, bearing N.E. distant 8 leagues; at noon Cape Chatham bore N.E ½ E.

distant 7 miles, and whales innumerable were playing around us in every direction.

October 8th.—At 8, A. M., Mount Gardner bore N.E. ½ E. distant 5 leagues, Cape Bald Head, N.E. distant 2 leagues, and Eclipse Islands, W.N.W., one mile. At 10, A. M., we were in the entrance of King George III. Sound, when the easternmost land in sight bore E. by N. distant 9 leagues, and Mount Gardner now bore N.E. by E. ½ E. distant 3½ leagues, and Bald Head W. by S. one mile. Seal Island, up the bay, soon came within our view, which is situated up towards and near to the head of the Sound. We now worked the ship up the Sound, with a moderate breeze ahead, and came to at anchor in eleven fathoms water, sandy bottom, abreast of the watering-place, which is at a fine sandy beach, extending almost continuously from the chop of Bald Head up to the head of the Sound or Bay. After furling the sails and clearing up decks, we hoisted out our boats, and Messrs. Stanton Brown, the supercargo, and S. Coles, with myself, made use of one of them and landed on this beautiful beach, near to the rivulet of excellent fresh water. Here we selected a spot over a green lawn, for the erection of our tent for the accommodation of those sick with the scurvy, and then sent Mr. Brown, the first officer, with the carpenter, his mates, and a gang, to erect the tent. As soon as this was effected we landed and placed our sick comfortably in it, to feast on the scurvy-grass, &c. They even, directly after the first day passed, showed convalescent symptoms. For a wild country, this is an excellent place for refreshments, and the natives appear very simple and harmless. It is convenient to good wood and watering, with an abundance of wild game, and a variety of excellent shell and scale fish. The various kinds are equal to any country: some of the rock-fish taken by us would weigh between twenty-five and thirty pounds; and those of the shell-fish, the oy sters, particularly, were of the most inviting quality.

While here we had variable winds and weather, with showers of rain, at intervals, and also occasional calms.

The natives visited us at the tent, on shore, in small parties, only from three to six at a time, freely bartering their uncouth stone hatchets and implements, &c., all except their arms, for knives, and trinkets, such as beads, bright metal buttons &c. On their visiting our officers and people at the tent, when they arrived within a few rods of the tent, they would stop and shout aloud, and as soon as answered by our people, would then lay aside their arms, consisting of spears and war-clubs, and make signs for ours to put aside their arms, muskets, &c.;—this being done, they would freely come up and join our men, and promptly proceed without fear or hesitation, to trading.

Having completed our wood and water, and our sick on shore having recovered to a state of fair health again, we then, agreeably to instructions, buried a bottle, at a designated spot on Seal Island, and prepared our ship for sea.

Friday, 21st of October, 1808.—We weighed our anchor and worked the ship out of the Sound, on our departure. At 4, P. M., Mount Gardner bore N.W. by W. and Bald Head Chop, or Cape, (all per compass,) W.N.W. distant 8 leagues, from which we took our departure.

King George III. Sound is free and clear of danger, in ingress or egress, and Bald Head Cape is such a remarkable head-land that it cannot be mistaken by the mariner, aided by the mark of Mount Gardner.

Wednesday, December 7th, 1808.—We came in sight of Eaoa, or Middleburgh Island, the centre of which I place in latitude 21° 23′ S. and longitude 175° 27′ W. of London. On the next day, we entered Van Diemen's Road, with the view of obtaining refreshments, when our ship was soon surrounded by a great number of ca noes, with numerous natives in them, as also on the beach. A brisk trade of barter now commenced, continuing until sun-down, for hogs, bread-fruit, yams, &c, &c., at which time we bore away and made sail for the Feejees. On the 10th of same month, the Island of Fatoa, or Turtle Island, was within our view, and our ship soon entered on this most intricate and most dangerous navigation ever undertaken by man, viz:—the Archipelago of the Feejees.

Sunday the 11*th*.—We arrived off abreast the main outer wall reef, in sight of Toconroba, the King's, or the Capital Island of the group. Late in the afternoon, we were visited by two young Princes, bringing some small presents of fruits, and to ascertain what ship it was, who was her commander, &c., &c. to report to the King. They were overjoyed when they learned whose ship it was, and that Mr. Brown, their adopted brother, was on board. His Majesty, they said, was well, and would be gratified beyond measure to see them, and had got our treaty cargo of sandal wood cut, shaved, and piled up on the small Island, already in waiting for us. Thus, in great haste, after completing their errand, and receiving from me a suitable return present, they left us almost in ecstasy, to carry the good news, with all despatch, to His Majesty, saying, that the King would visit our ship in the morning. This assurance was confirmed by an earnest remark at the moment they departed in their large and highly ornamented canoe, for the shore.

During the night a number of fires or lights were seen by us, from on board the ship, in different parts on the land, which we concluded were to give light to the natives in their work of gathering fruits, yams, &c., for a barter trade with us. This subsequently proved to be the fact, as very early in the morning the ship was surrounded by numerous canoes, large and small, which brought off to us an abundance of hogs, bread-fruit, yams, cocoa nuts, &c. The yams had the dirt fresh upon them, and corroborated the assertion of the natives, affording conclusive evidence, that they had been pulled during the night by the lights, as we had conjectured.

When morning came, at 8, A. M., a fleet of war canoes in great state appeared in sight, steering for the ship. On inquiring of the natives, now trading with us, they informed us, that the fleet was coming with their King,

Tynahoa, to pay a visit to the captain of our ship. His Majesty was soon within our view, seated on the platform or deck of the double, large, war canoe, under an awning, in great state, accompanied by the two young Princes, who had paid their respects to us last evening; and also surrounded by a few of his principal chiefs. On their coming alongside the ship, a scene was presented before our eyes, which, I believe, moved the feelings of every individual on board of her, as well as the chiefs in attendance on His Majesty. I met and received His Majesty with congratulations, on the forepart of my quarter deck, and, after the necessary friendly salutations, I stepped aside, introducing his former adopted son, Mr. Brown. The King instantly encircled him in his arms, as if a child, when one minute passed, and another, and yet another—His Majesty seemingly too much absorbed by his feelings to be willing to slack up his embrace—with the continued expressions, "My son! my son!" The large, pearly drops rolled down his cheeks, and he was, to all appearance, quite overjoyed, and affectionately unmanned in again meeting with his adopted son! This scene seemed, apparently, not only to petrify our officers and men, as they gazed on it, but also the natives, fixing them, like statues, on the deck.

The King spent an hour on board in making inquiries, &c., and informing me that he had kept and fulfilled our treaty faithfully thus far, and that the like full faith, on his part, should be continued to the end. This proved to be correct, as the sequel will show.

Several English vessels, it seems, from Port Jackson, had been there after sandal wood, &c., and for trade during my absence, two of which were now lying at anchor in the harbour, waiting for the Taboo (prohibition) to be raised; but not a tree had been disposed of; and farther, agreeably to the faith of said treaty, a full ship's cargo was now prepared and piled on the island, ready for me. This, the King said, should be brought by his chiefs alongside, and delivered, on board of my ship, as soon as I should desire, after our ship should be anchored in Sandal Wood Harbour, or Road. Then, after welcoming us over and over, and presenting me with a very large, fat hog, yams, cocoa-nuts, and bread-fruits, and receiving, in return, a suitable (so here considered,) royal present from me, with that also brought for him by his adopted son, and obtaining positive assurance from me, that his son, Mr. Brown, should be at liberty to repair on shore, at His Majesty's residence, immediately after the ship was brought at anchor in the harbour, His Majesty and court attendants departed for the shore.

After sailing through the narrow passage of the main reef, and bringing our ship to anchor in the harbour of Sandal Wood Bay, Mr. Brown promptly, and agreeably to our understanding, went on shore, to the King's residence, and remained there the most of the time during our stay. As soon as His Majesty was informed that our ship was ready, his chiefs commenced bringing the wood frcm the island alongside; but nevertheless, as they would, in spite of all our coaxing and persuasion, take it leisurely, in their own way and time, and as they had their wars and feasts to attend to, we were delayed until the month of March, before the cargo could be all shipped and on board. However, as some consolation for this delay, the King had complied bountifully, for we had to stow our launch in her chocks full, and also to take a quantity on deck, to receive all on board which he had provided.

This being now accomplished, the Royal prohibition, or Taboo, by His Majesty's proclamation, through his chiefs, was raised, or taken off, to the great relief and gladness of those waiting in the other vessels, which had been so long here in tried patience, waiting to purchase. Trade with all comers was now again freely per mitted.

Full supplies of fuel, water, with a plentiful sea stock of hogs, fowls, yams, bread-fruits, &c., being received on board, and after, as I believe, a truly friendly and affectionate parting with the King and his sons, the young Princes, who had got strongly attached to us, and a promise, (which no presents, or argumentative sayings, could put aside,) to return again in eighteen moons, if our owners should so decide and direct:—being now ready, we cleared up ship to sail and proceed to sea.

CHAPTER II.

Ship departs from the Feejees—Remarks on the passage to sea—Ship takes a new route for China—Meets with much drift wood, &c.—Discover the Tonquin Islands—Pass Dough's Group—Volcano Island—Its columns of smoke—Discover the Group of Equator Isles—Signs of Inhabitants—Discover an extensive and important Group of Islands, to which they give the name of American Group—Dangerous situation of the ship—Arrival at Canton—Sail for New-York—Arrival.

Thursday, 21*st of March*, 1809.—We proceeded with the ship through the pass in the main wall reef, and took our departure from the Feejees.

REMARKS.—On the passage to sea, from the anchorage at Sandal Wood Road, by the way or pass, by Union Point,—(note, that all bearings and courses are taken by compass,)—having Union Point bearing E. about one mile distant, (which is a small point south of Corobata, distant from it three miles,) then direct your course W.S.W. for nine or ten miles, which will bring the body of the Islands of Antua, (which are situated very close together,) to bear north, distant between two and three miles from your ship; then steer west, and if it be now clear weather, you will soon see the Island of Levo Callow, bearing W.N.W. This island cannot be mistaken for any other island, as there is no other on the starboard hand, after leaving Antua. Levo Callow may be seen ten leagues off, appears round and even on the top, and is about a mile in circumference. When Levo Callow bears N.W., you will see Bligh's Island, (called by the natives, Assava,) ahead on your larboard bow. Bligh's Island is long and low, excepting one high peak about its middle, the east end extending out to within about eight miles of Levo Callow. One mile N.E. from this end or point, lie two small islands, surrounded with reefs; your officer on the look-out at the mast head, will plainly see them, when running down from Antua. There is also, as will be seen, an extensive range of reefs, which put out from that island, quite down to Levo Callow. Be careful to give this reef, or range, a good berth, as there are straggling rocks, or small patches of reef out at some considerable distance from its main range. The Ship Hope ran over one of these patches, but, by good fortune, did not touch. In the Tonquin, by our sharp look-out, and close attention, we did but just escape running our ship on one of them.

Continue your course west until Levo Callow bears north, which carries you clear of all the reefs and dangers; then steer north by west, or N. by W. ½ W., keeping Levo Callow on your starboard hand. You may pass within a mile of it, in a fine clear channel of five or six miles broad, leading to sea. After passing with the Tonquin through this channel, at 6, P. M. we took our depature from Levo Callow, it bearing S.E. by E. distant three miles, and being situated in latitude 15° 47′ south, longitude, 175° 41′ east of London We now took and steered on a new and untraversed route for China.

Saturday, April 1st, 1809.—We passed a considerable quantity of drift-wood and Mangrove nuts, our latitude being, at the time, 14° 15′ south.

Wednesday, 5th of April, 1809.—At 6, A. M. that ever-pleasing sound to the mariner and others, on long passages, and more especially to us, now far from home, was heard from the look-out aloft, of "Land, ho!" which proved to be an extensive island, or islands, and I regretted much that my instructions and time did not allow me to make an examination. Being a new discovery, I gave the name Tonquin Islands to the land, which, at noon, bore N.E. by E., distant 6 leagues. The centre of this Island or Islands, (as there is an opening which, at our distance, had the appearance of a ship water passage between the Islands, or lands, and a small spiral rocky Islet lay at a short distance to the northward of the northernmost land,) we place in latitude 11° 52′ south, and longitude 169° 44′ east of London; variation 11° 20′ east.

Thursday, 6th of April.—At 9, A. M., we had sight of another small Island, in latitude 11° 24′ S., longitude 167° 06′ 15″ E. to which we gave the name of Palm Tree Island.

Saturday, the 8th—We had a distant view of Dough's Group, or Swallow Islands, and passed them at the distance of 6 or 7 leagues. At meridian, saw Volcano Island, which I place in latitude 10° 12′ south, longitude 164° 50′ east, variation 9° 50′ east, we observed columns of smoke continually issuing from its summit and ascending to a great elevation, by which and its height, this Island, or its situation, by its volcanic smoke, can be seen in clear weather, at least sixty miles, by a man at the mast head of an ordinary sized merchant ship.

April 12th.—In latitude 7° 23′ south, passed much drift wood, Mangrove nuts, &c., with patches of rock weed, as the ship sailed along on her course steering to the north-westward.

April 25th.—Just at the morning's broad day-light, we were treated again with the welcome sound of "Land, ho!" from the masthead, bearing N.½E., distant 5 miles, which proved to be a number of small low islands, to appearance only eight or ten feet above the surface of the sea, but covered with tall cocoanut trees. They can be seen therefore in clear weather only, about as far as a grove of cocoanut trees could be seen on the surface of Neptune's element. Still, as we passed them, it was evident, that they were inhabited, as many smokes were made which ascended aloft, and continued rising as we passed the whole length, or range of the cluster. It was only about the extent of three miles, tending east and west.

Considering them to be a new discovery, we named them Equator Isles; they are situated, in latitude 00° 57′ north, longitude 155_0 19′ east.

Sunday, 30*th April*, 1809.—Not dreaming of being near to any coast, our surprise was very great, when the loud voice at the look-out at the top-mast head, at half-past 4, P. M., shouted, "Land, ho!" bearing right-a-head direct in our course, and off each bow. When the next half hour thereafter had passed, it was extensively seen bearing and extending from N.E. around by the north, and westward to the W.S.W. I now immediately caused the ship to be brought to the wind, with her head to the southward, which owing to a strong gale now blowing from the south-eastward and nearly direct on the land, with hard squalls, brought her instantly under close-reefed topsails. The land now appeared to consist of a number, or chain of islands, and the southernmost seen by us in the evening at dusk, was but a very short distance from the ship. After the night had closed upon us, making our view around very limited indeed, we could, notwithstanding, distinctly see the land between the heavy squalls, which with the tremendous sea rolling on, caused our very excellent ship, a truly first-rate seaboat, under her heavy press of canvass, to labour hard, as she struggled with it, to keep off this strange shore; we were forced to keep on her this absolutely necessary press of canvass to enable her to keep clear of this strange land, whose coast was now, so close a neighbour to us. In our dangerous situation it could not possibly be dispensed with; to add to our very trying situation, and to save the masts from being torn from their steps overboard, we were obliged by 9, P. M., by the increased gale, and added violence of the squalls, in order to save our masts and spars, notwithstanding our increased danger, and the constant weight of the most painful anxiety on the mind, to furl our topsails, and to bring our well-behaved ship under her reefed courses, with the storm-staysails. At about 10, P. M., just as we had began to think ourselves clear of danger from the coast, and its shore,—on a sudden, between the squalls, the land appeared again bearing about west from us. Though at great risk of losing our masts and canvass I was brought under the severe trial, and absolute necessity of ordering the close-reefed top sails to be set again upon our now over-pressed, and most superior behaved boat. As she plunged, and ploughed through the raging and foaming element, she trembled with her load of pressure like an aspen-leaf in the breeze;

but our really dangerous situation, the giant sea, the weather, and the violent gale were such, that there was no alternative,—it was life or death. It pleased, however, the Almighty, and blessed Saviour of man, to permit our ship to clear this newly-discovered promontory and coast, on which hung our destiny. As soon as this was effected, we relieved our well-behaved boat, by again furling the fore and mizen topsails,—and were employed manœuvring our ship to traverse over as small a space of ground during the remainder of the night as possible. At half past 5, A. M., the land was again seen close under our lee; we immediately set again the close-reefed fore and mizen-topsails to endeavour to clear it, and as the day lighted up, more and extensive land came within our view, in its present appearance like a thick cluster of islands, tending about E. by N., and W. by S. After the sun was risen, upwards of twenty islands were counted within the range of our view from the mast-head, at the same time breakers were also seen between all the nearest ones, which were now distant about three miles from the ship. These are a dangerous and extensive group of low islands, chained in appearance together by coral reefs, and rocks above water. Their extent from east to west (as far as came within our view) is about fifteen leagues. The south-side of the range, on which our ship was, in form appeared somewhat like a crescent. Thus having passed through one of the most trying and anxious nights that can happen to a commander, or to man, we now bore up to the westward, and proceeded along and around the west-end of the westernmost island, as we judged it to be, for as we passed it there was no land to be seen in the western board from aloft. Concluding them a new discovery, we called them the American Group. Their centre I judge to be, and place in latitude of 5° 3′ north, longitude 152° 25′ east of London.

The very unpleasant weather and want of time, did not give us an opportunity, to examine the islands of the American Group by a landing, which I much regretted, as I was very desirous of obtaining more particulars; but I did not feel that the loss of time to obtain them, by effecting a landing, would justify it with my duty. We saw no signs of these islands being inhabited.

After this discovery nothing unusual occurred to us during the remainder of this voyage; and the author thinking that the daily sea account of remarks, would not be sufficiently amusing and entertaining to the reader, for insertion, omits it, and respectfully closes the narrative, by merely stating, that after arriving at Canton, and exchanging their cargo for China goods, the Tonquin proceeded and arrived safe, all well, at the port of New-York, with her full cargo of teas, and other China goods. From this cargo, an amount of some thousands of dollars for duties was paid into the national treasury.

It is thus, by the constant, repeated, similar, and many voyages under the command, or directive agency of the author, that he has been the means; by those articles of trade so highly prized by the Chinese, and procured at lands, &c., in the South Seas, and Pacific oceans; of bringing large amounts into the national treasury, amounting in the aggregate to millions of dollars, as well as enriching his fellow-citizens, and adding much wealth to his country, since the year 1792. The date of his early move, was the first to discover and open the way to this valuable commercial trade to his enterprising countrymen. His voluntary, persevering exertions, to obtain the authorization by congress of the present National American South Sea Exploring Expedition to endeavour to revive and advance this nearly obsolete, but valuable trade, &c., has been to him a sacrifice of above three thousand dollars, exclusive of time, in travel, and in personal attendance on the several sessions of congress,—and as he has never yet received a dollar from government for services, or otherwise; he therefore hopes, when the author is no longer among the living, that a generous public will thereafter award to him, and his relatives, the credit of a worthy citizen, and real friend to mankind, his country's commerce, navigation, &c. If this laudable National South-Sea Exploring Expedition, now authorized, and fitting out, which the author has so arduously toiled for to be sent out by government, be not ably and successfully conducted, and carried through to a favourable, beneficial, and brillant result, it will be *no* fault of his. Time alone can decide, while we hope for the best.

CHAPTER III.

Narrative of the Massacre of the crew of the American ship Tonquin, under the command of Lieutenant J. Thorn, U S. Navy, by the savages of the north-west coast of America, and the destruction of the ship.

SECTION I.

Tonquin anchors in Neweatee harbour—Visited by the natives—Brisk fur trade—Affront of an aged chief—Savage threat of revenge—Trade interrupted—Natives quit the ship—Natives revisit the ship, in unusual numbers—Interpreter discovers the natives on deck to be secretly armed—Their horrid war-yell—The attack and massacre—Captain Thorn, the clerk, and four seamen regain the ship's deck—Savages driven from the ship—Slaughter of the savages, and destruction of their canoes by the ship's fire—Four seamen quit the ship—Natives are induced to again visit the ship—Ship's decks crowded with numerous savages—Ship blown up by Captain Thorn—Terrible scene of destruction—The four seamen taken by the savages and cruelly put to death.

OTHER versions* of the very lamentable death of the gallant and brave Thorn, having appeared, the author of these voyages deems it but justice due to the honour and credit of the gallant officers of our navy, that they, as well as the relatives and friends of the brave Thorn,

* See Irving's Astoria, vol. I. page 116.

should have every report how, and in what manner, this determined and noble spirited officer of the United States navy perished, with the mysterious destruction of his ship. As an introduction, the author would, with all respect, remark, That after the return of the Tonquin from her late voyage to the Feejees, and Canton, (see the preceding pages) she was sold to John Jacob Astor, Esq., a highly respected and wealthy merchant of the city of New-York, for an enterprising voyage to the north-west coast of America. The following narrative will show the fatal end of this beautiful and very valuable ship.

Captain James P. Sheffield, in the Brig Hersilia, of Stonington,* being on a trading voyage and cruise in 1823 and 24, on the coast of California, informed the author, that he employed on board his vessel an Indian fellow, by the name of Lamayzie, who told Captain Sheffield, that he was interpreter and pilot of the Ship Tonquin, Captain J. Thorn, when the horrid massacre of her crew took place, and the ship was blown up.

* This, the second Hersilia belonging to the South-Sea Company, was built by the order of their agent, the author, to replace the one that was captured by Beneviades, and wrecked at Arauco, on coast of Chili.—See page — of this volume.

He then gave to Captain Sheffield the following narrative of this melancholy and bloody occurrence. The following are the particulars as received by the author from Captain Sheffield.

HISTORICAL NARRATIVE.

The Tonquin, on her trading voyage along the north-west coast, had anchored in Neweatee harbour, at English, or Vancouver Island. Soon after anchoring the ship, Mr. Mackay, the supercargo, went on shore, to the principal chief's village, to pay a visit to the head chief Wycananish, a half dozen petty chiefs remaining on board of the Tonquin as hostages for his safe return. The supercargo was very kindly received by this chief and the natives, well treated, and remained at the village all night, not returning on board until the early part of the next day. In the meantime, and very early in the morning, the natives came off to the ship in numbers in their canoes, headed by two sons of the principal chief, with an aged chief in company, bringing a large quantity of sea-otter skins and other furs, affording the prospect of a good and profitable trade, and seemingly with every friendly disposition. Captain Thorn permitted them to come freely on deck in any numbers, and spread his articles of trade profusely out before them. Captain Thorn thinking, by the abundance of rich furs now brought so promptly off by the natives, to buy cheap, with this view set off a smaller proportion of articles to each otter skin, &c., than was usually given by the American traders in this barter; which being observed by the old chief, who had some experience in this barter trade, with the previous American vessels, he in a rapid vocabulary of words, interfered and stopped the natives from trading. This much exasperated the captain, and induced him to treat the old chief very roughly, forcing him out of the ship down the gangway into his canoe. The old savage was rendered by this act wildly mad, and left the ship with terrible threats; the two young chiefs also, and all the natives (except the hostages) promptly quitted the ship, with their furs for the shore. Thereupon the interpreter took the liberty to observe to the captain, that he would advise him to endeavour to pacify the old chief, and to take some measure to bring him on friendly terms again, as it was a pity to lose the prospect of such a good trade; but the captain treated the suggestion with contempt, as he briskly walked the deck, appearing to be in rather a violent passion. When Mr. Mackay, the supercargo, returned on board, the pilot related to him what had occurred, and in what fury the old chief had left the ship, desiring him to use his endeavour to persuade the captain to get the ship immediately under way, and leave the harbour, as he was sure, knowing the Indian disposition and feelings, that this aged chief would not peaceably put up with such an affront.

The supercargo on learning this, went immediately to the captain, who was yet quickly pacing the deck back and forth. and used his best endeavours, by earnest entreaty and advice, to persuade him to leave this anchorage, but all in vain, the captain ridiculed his advice, and said, he would pacify the savage, and his tribe with the battery on his deck. The remainder of the day passed away without any movement on the part of the natives, and at the usual hour in the evening, the captain and supercargo retired to their berths, leaving the mates to attend to and regulate the watch for the night, as had been previously and usually arranged.

At the dawn of day on the next morning, a small canoe with two natives and a squaw came cautiously alongside the ship. Being friendly received by the officer of the deck-watch, in the command of the deck, they again soon returned to the shore, when a large canoe, with a young chief, a son of their head-chief, with about twenty natives, bringing with them a good lot of sea-otter skins, came alongside, to trade, all, to outward appearance, unarmed, and with many friendly signs, indicative of a desire for a brisk trade. Other canoes soon followed off to the ship, and as no orders to the contrary had been before given out, the officer in the command of the deck permitted the savages to come freely on board, until such an increased number had got on the decks, and around the ship, that he became alarmed, and directed the captain and supercargo to be called up. When they came on deck, the captain declined to order the ship's decks to be cleared of the natives, but directed the brisk, and as he no doubt thought innocent and advantageous trade to be continued, when, in a short time, he himself became uneasy by the numerous additional canoes and natives continually coming off from the shore to the ship At this time, the interpreter, having discovered that the savages came on board armed, with their short war-clubs, and Indian daggers, secreted under their mantles, or short skin cloaks, he immediately but cautiously informed the captain of it; who, without first clearing the ship's decks of the natives, gave orders to get the ship under way, sending some seamen to the windlass to heave up the anchor, and some aloft to loose the sails. The seamen had but just got at work at their stations (the trade at the same time going on in hurry and bustle) when the savages gave the war-whoop, flourished their war-clubs and daggers, and the murderous attack then commenced. The first victim, the Indian said he saw struck, was the clerk, a young man, by name Lewis, with a stroke by a dagger, in the back part of the neck, when he fell against the side of the companion-way, down on the gangway steps. On soon coming to himself, he closed and bolted the companion way doors, and retreated to the cabin. The skylight of the quarter-deck had been previously taken off and removed to pass up goods and articles for trade. At this moment the captain, badly daggered and mortally wounded, fell down through it into the cabin. The captain, who was a brave and determined man, of superior strength, at the time of the first war-whoop, was standing on the quarter-deck, just forward of the mizen-mast. Observing a powerful chief coming upon him, with drawn dagger, he drew his large dirk that he had of late kept constantly at his waist, and with one plunge thrust it into the breast of the savage, and laid him dead at his feet; but being now set upon by numbers, he received several wounds from their daggers, and was forced back against the steering wheel-frame, when a savage behind him gave him a blow on the back of the head and neck, with a war-club, which knocked him over, and, as before mentioned, down through the skylight opening into the cabin for dead, as then supposed, aside of Mr. Lewis. At the time of the first savage-yell, Mr. Mackay, the supercargo, was on the ship's tafferel, and immediately sprung forward to assist the captain, when he was knocked down by a blow of the war-club given by an herculean savage, and immediately pierced with many daggers, and thrown overboard, where the remnant of his life was soon destroyed by the squaws in their canoes. The pilot, at this time, moved himself out over the tafferel on one of the boat's stern-davids, where he remained until he saw, as he then thought, all the officers, and men massacred, except those aloft, and the savages in complete possession of the decks, when he lowered himself down by the boat's tackle into a canoe, where he soon heard the report of pistols, which, he subsequently learned, were fired by the clerk from out of the cabin skylight, under the counsel of the captain, at those savages on the quarter-deck. This soon cleared this deck of them, when the clerk called to the seamen aloft;

(the main-hatches as well as cover to the sky-light, having been previously taken off, to pass up goods for trade,) to lower themselves down by a rope, from the main-stay into the hatch-way, and then come aft to the cabin, on which they took the studding-sail halyards from the maintop and making the bight fast to the main-stay, dropped the two ends into the main hatch-way, when they slid one at a time down by the end-parts into the hatch-way, and between decks, and aft into the cabin. The first three, to the surprise of the natives on the main-deck, got safely down and into the cabin; but the savages having now awaked from their amaze-ment, attacked and massacred the last three, when they descended. The one in the mizen-top having made fast a line to the gaft over the skylight, and the savages having been already driven from the quarter-deck by the fire of Mr. Lewis, the clerk, under direction of the captain, who was yet unable to stand on his feet, the seaman then slid down by his line into the ca-bin, without danger or hurt; and he, being the first one aloft which thus acted, gave encou-ragement to his shipmates in the main and foretops to promptly follow his example, and proceed as related.

There being now four seamen unhurt in the cabin with the mortally wounded captain and clerk to direct and assist them, and plenty of loaded muskets and pistols at hand, they mounted on the table, under the skylight which brought their heads and shoulders, just above the deck, and commenced a brisk fire of musketry at the savages on the maindeck. This soon cleared it of those bloody murderers, when Mr. Lewis and the four seamen repaired to their battery, and let off the loaded cannon upon them and their canoes, which caused terrible slaughter, destroying many of their canoes and thus affording to those remaining alive on board, peaceable possession of their ship again. In the general battle the officers and men had fought with a determined courage, but were overpowered by crowded numbers. Lamayzie, the pilot, on withdrawing by sliding down the tackle in his retreat into their canoe, and having given no assistance in the fight, was considered by the natives as a neutral, and by them treated as such. After all that remained alive of these wild murderers, had got again on shore, out of reach and fear of the deck-guns, not an individual of them left it again during the remainder of the day, and the night passed in peace. When morning came, the ship was seen still at anchor with her sails loose, when the interpreter was desired to go off to her with some natives in a large canoe, to which, suiting his mind, he readily consented. They paddled off cautiously around the ship, when Mr. Lewis appearing on deck, called to them to come on board, making at the same time friendly signs, that they had nothing to fear, and on proceeding alongside and meeting with no opposition, they very readily sprang on deck, which was yet covered with heaps of goods, articles of trade exposed the previous day. Mr. Lewis directed the interpreter to say to the natives, that they might take and divide all the goods on deck among themselves, only now be at peace and friendly. This being made known, numbers of canoes came off, bringing the natives and squaws, in unusual numbers, and thus crowding the ship's decks, and also hanging on her sides around her. The clerk now invited the interpreter into the cabin, where he saw Captain Thorn sitting on the after locker, with a lighted match in his hand. He looked very pale, and was near the magazine scuttle, by which on the cabin deck, was a large heap of gun-powder, and two oakum ropes covered with the same, leading from the heap into the magazine. Mr. Lewis gave an explanation relative to what had passed on the day before and during the night, and then said to him, "You see the captain can't live long, and is going to blow up the ship with all these barbarian murderers about her, and as I myself cannot long survive, I am going with him." He then told him if he wished to live, not to speak a single word, but to take a roll of cloth, and bunch of beads, and immediately to lower himself out at the cabin window, and repair to some canoe and promptly move off, and not to speak until he was in it, for if he did, that instant he spoke, the ship would be blown up. He acted accordingly, and swam to a canoe having in it two squaws. Showing them the beads, they very readily received him into their canoe, quickly paddling her safe out from among the fleet, to keep the prize, which he had brought. On looking back to the ship, he saw Mr. Lewis looking out of the cabin window after him; and, on his drawing himself in and disappearing, immediately the ship blew up with a terrible explosion, destroying a great number of savages and herself disappearing. He saw nothing more after this of Captain Thorn, nor Mr. Lewis, but thought it best and most judicious to keep to himself the secret given to him while in the cabin. The squaws in the canoe which had received him, proved to be the wives of a chief of some influence, who had had the good fortune to have come out of this bloody slaughtering affair unscathed, and with whom the beads and roil of blue cloth paved the way, and obtained a peaceable home for him at their residence in the village. The bay now showed on its surface a horrid sight, strewed over with yelling, wounded savages, floating parts of the blown up ship, with shattered portions of wrecked canoes. To these were added the mourning, savage, wailing howls of the escaped natives and women of the village.

The four unhurt seamen had embarked in the ship's small boat, in the night, with the hope of getting back in her to the settlement the ship had previously made at the mouth of Columbia River, but were forced on shore by the strong wind and current, and the next day were discovered and taken prisoners by the natives, and immediately brought to the village, where the interpreter spoke with them, and learned their views and intentions, on quitting the ship. To this step they said, they were mainly induced by the fear and expectation, that they in the ship would be attacked during the night, and overpowered by hosts of the savages, and also massacred; but, alas! poor fellows, they were now in a much worse and more dreadful situation. They were all put to death by cruel, lingering torture, in the usual horrid manner of savages.

Thus, it seems, by placing too much confidence in these wild savages, awfully perished the brave and daring Thorn, and the whole of the twenty-two persons under his charge. Thus also ended the career of this fine ship, the Tonquin, and with her all the promising prospects of the voyage were destroyed,—deplorably showing of how little real service is ability and talent, even of no ordinary kind, unless combined with that wisdom which dwells with prudence.

SECTION II.

A List of newly discovered Lands in the South Seas and Pacific, with their situations.

Farnham's Island, discovered by Bolivar, Liberator, in 1833. Latitude 14° 46′ north, longitude 169° 18′ east. Six miles long, tending W.N.W. and E.S E.

Ladd's Island, discovered by Missionary Packet, in 1834. Latitude 17° 26′ north, longitude 133° 15′ west.

Michell Island, discovered by the Mary Michell, in 1834. Latitude 11° 30′ south, longitude 165° 35′ west. A low island, about two miles long, and full of wood.

Barstow Island, discovered by the Gideon Barstow, in 1834. Latitude 23° 12′ south, longitude 137° 24′ west.

Leavitt's Island, discovered by the Peruvian, April 12th, 1835 Latitude 10° 4′ south, longitude 152° 25′ west. This Island has a white sandy beach, and is covered with trees.

New-Port Island, discovered by ship Audley Clark, Captain Paddock, on December 28th, 1836. Thickly wooded, but no appearance of its being inhabited. Latitude 11° 37′ south, longitude 162° 25′ west.

Acteon's Islands, discovered January, 1831. Three Islands compose the group.	Lat. 21° 29′ S. lon. 136° 27′ W.
	" 21° 23′ S. " 136° 32′ W.
	" 21° 19′ S. " 136° 38′ W.

Raraka Island, 1¼ leagues in extent. Latitude 15° 52′ south, longitude 144° 47′ west.

Single Island, very low above the surface of the sea. Latitude 16° 5′ south, longitude 130° 41′ west.

Michell's Group, their presumed centre, in latitude 31° 27′ S.
Supposed longitude of their eastern extreme, 130° 41′ W.

PART V.

EXTRACTS FROM THE MEMORIALS TO CONGRESS, PRAYING THAT A NATIONAL DISCOVERY AND EXPLORING EXPEDITION BE AUTHORIZED, AND SENT OUT TO THE SOUTH SEAS, PACIFIC OCEAN, &c., WITH A STATEMENT OF THE PROBABLE NATIONAL BENEFITS IN VIEW, &c., &c., THAT MAY BE OBTAINED, BY PERFORMING SUCH AN EXPEDITION, WITH NOTES EXPLANATORY OF THE SUBJECT.

The following extracts are from memorials by the author, which were presented at the Session of Congress, in 1831, and also at subsequent dates, and were continued with urgent zeal, and supported by memorials from numerous highly respectable citizens of New-York, Philadelphia, &c., &c., up to the time said National Exploring Expedition was by Congress authorized:—

EXTRACT FROM THE MEMORIAL

OF

EDMUND FANNING,

Presented to Congress, praying that a National Discovery and Exploring Expedition be sent out to the South Seas, &c., December, 1831.

Referred to the Committee on Naval Affairs, and ordered to be printed.

To the Honourable the Senate and House of Representatives of the United States, in Congress assembled:—

Your petitioner, Edmund Fanning, having obtained satisfactory evidence, by the trial and result, that any private exploring expedition cannot ever produce, or obtain, the desired and wished-for national benefit to navigation, commercial trade, the whale and seal fishery, science, &c.; therefore, under a full acquired belief of its national importance, impressed as your memorialist is, by personal experience, in the necessity of a governmental exploring expedition to those parts of our globe, doth, in his national feeling and zeal, and in all humble deference, most respectfully recommend and pray, that Congress, in its wisdom, will be pleased to grant an appropriation, with power for a competent National Exploring and Discovery Expedition to the South Seas, Pacific, &c. In aid and support of which recommendation, your memorialist has heretofore made sundry discoveries in those seas, and had long and much experience relating to the subject. And your memorialist, as in duty bound, will ever pray.

EDMUND FANNING.

New-York, Nov. 7th, 1831.

23d Congress.) (1st Session.

MEMORIAL

OF

EDMUND FANNING,

To illustrate the views in a petition presented to Congress, praying that a National Discovery and Exploring Expedition be sent out to the South Seas, &c. December 18th, 1833.

Referred to the committee on naval affairs, and ordered to be printed.

To the Honourable the Senate and House of Representatives of the United States, in Congress assembled:—

EXTRACTS FROM THIS CONTINUED MEMORIAL, &c.

Your petitioner, Edmund Fanning, respectfully asketh leave to submit the following explanations, reasons, &c., to illustrate his views of the national advantages and benefits prayed for, in his petition before Congress, and on file with your honourable committee, that a national discovery and exploring expedition be sent out to the South Seas, &c., &c.; and does also farther respectfully request, that the said explanations, remarks, &c., with his former petition, and papers attached thereto, on file with your honourable naval committee, may be again printed. Your petitioner, in all deference, requests leave to observe, that, at the early date of 1792, he entered and engaged on those South Sea voyages, with a view to obtain information on the seal fishery, commercial trade, pecuniary profit, &c., that which at this time was thought might be obtained from those foreign ports and unexplored regions.

In 1797, your memorialist sailed on his voyage, in the capacity of commander, supercargo, and director, to prosecute this commercial trade and seal fishery, to the South Seas, Pacific Ocean, China, and around the world. This new and enterprising voyage opened the gate to his fellow-citizens to this South Pacific and China commercial trade; by which, and thereafter, under his command or agency, were taken from these regions to China, on American account, the first cargoes of sandal wood, seals, fur, beach-la-mer, bird's nest, mother of pearl, pearls, sharks' fins, turtle shell, &c., being the productions of the lands, seas, in those South Sea and Pacific regions; which, on being exchanged in Canton, for China goods, and those brought home into our ports of the United States, not only enriched his brother citizens, the adventurers, but poured streams, by duties on the same, of hundreds of thousands, ay, millions of dollars, into the public treasury, thus enriching our country in the aggregate; and which, in the course of some few years, therefore, caused this commercial traffic and fishery to increase to upwards of twenty sail per annum, out of the ports of the United States, and which has now got dwindled down to a very limited number: In your petitioner's next voyage to the South Seas, the Pacific, China, and around the world, he was honoured in the command of a superb new corvette ship, of 22 guns, commissioned by the President of the United States, with a complement of five lieutenants, a master, a surgeon, eight midshipmen, with a competent number of petty officers and men, which voyage was also safely performed around the world, without any unpleasant occurrence or difficulty, but in good discipline, harmony, &c. And having, during his voyages in the command and directing agency, had the fortune to discover the group of Fanning's Islands, Palmyrie Island, Washington Island, (so named on its discovery by the subscriber, a beautiful green island that stands recorded on the charts in use, by this name of the father of our country) Border's Island, as also, the continent of Palmer's Land, and rediscovered the group of Crozett's Islands, the South-Antipode's Island, were the first Americans at the Feejee Islands, and to the new South-Shetland Islands:—from all of which there has been produced much wealth to our beloved country, as well as to its national treasury;—were the first from among our enterprising fellow-citizens, that took from those regions and seas, on American account to China, those products of sandal wood, &c., &c., which then, as before-mentioned, being exchanged in Canton for silks, nankins, teas, &c., &c., (China goods,) not only produced large profits to the adventurers, but also enriched the national treasury. And in the utmost respect the subscriber hereunto would remark:—Do not these discoveries and their effects, with the millions of wealth which this trade and fishery have heretofore brought into our country, by its enterprizing citizens, and also to its national treasury, have a parental claim on government for a competent exploring and discovery expedition, to endeavour now to revive it again?

And to revive this commercial trade, fishery, &c., as well as to obtain other important national benefits, I do now most respectfully and earnestly petition and pray Congress, for this discovery and exploring expedition to be sent out, to explore and search out new resources, or places, to obtain those products, articles, &c., which places, it is confidently conceived and believed, are yet numerous to be found, and thereby the said products will be again obtained in plenty, when those contemplated new places of resort, &c., are discovered and marked down on the chart, by this exploring, *with proper vessels*, on such national service.

Presuming your petitioner's information, by such lengthy experience, to be equal to that of any other, and that your petitioner has had the fortune to do as much, if not more, than any other citizen, in searching out and bringing forward those national advantages and benefits touching on the before-mentioned business of commercial trade, &c., to the South Seas, Pacific, and China, as well as by first opening the gate-way to the prosecuting this valuable fishery and commercial trade, which has so enriched the national treasury, and brought such wealth to his fellow-citizens, which your petitioner conceives, in all due deference, entitles him to, and gives to him the firm ground of confidence, and of claim to respectfully ask, by his said petition, of our nation's Congress, the granting it, by the authorizing the prosecu tion of this national project.

But laying aside, for a moment, this Pacific and China commercial trade, your memorialist would observe, adverting to the subject, that the whale and seal fishery to the South Seas, of late years, has increased in the number of vessels beyond that of any former time, from out of the ports of the United States, and are still on the increase:—therefore the more urgency there is now of this national exploration, in the immediate need to its support:—Also in further illustration, as touching on the seal and whale fisheries, history gives to us the fact, that the British Greenland Whale and Seal Fishery at their old fishing grounds, had got reduced in their fleet engaged in this business, by the scarcity of the whales and seals, from upwards of eighty sail, down to a very limited number;—when the exploring and discovery voyages sent out by their government, under captains Ross and Parry, having discovered new fishing grounds, never before having been disturbed, up Davis' Straits, Baffin's Bay, &c., where the whales and seals were plenty, or numerous, revived again this fishery to such a degree, that they now have, annually, a fleet of between ninety and a hundred sail employed again in it, (which revival would undoubtedly have been lost to that nation, had not those exploring and discovery voyages been performed,) with renewed advantages, not only in bringing wealth to the nation, but in also establishing an additional nursery for seamen, which, it is well known, is the main spring of a navy.

And your memorialist is now in possession of the fact, that losing voyages by our American vessels have already, and lately, been made, owing to the scarcity of fishes and animals at their old grounds, or places of resort, for their requisite, natural, and annual wants of feed, propagation, &c.; particularly the latter, *the seals;* which ill success and hard fortune will still prevail, and in an increased measure, if not to a total abandonment in a few years, if this national exploring and research are not soon entered upon and effected, by discovering, marking down, and promulgating new resorts, grounds, and places, where those amphibious animals and fishes are to be again found in plenty, as they are still met with, numerous, on their travels, in those seas.

The vessels now employed in this whaling and sealing business to the South Seas, Pacific Ocean, &c., on taking their departure from our ports, proceed direct for the old grounds and places of resort of those fishes and animals where they are now found and met with, so scattering and wild as to protract their voyages, often to such a length as to frequently exhaust their provisions, which were laid in for the voyage; and, of course, oblige them to recruit in a foreign port, or force them to return home with a losing voyage, and which, it is confidently believed, such an exploration would prevent, and cause a more sure, prompt, and successful voyage and return, by its discovery and marking down of new grounds and places of their resorts:—which expedition would also make more sure and safe the life of the mariner, by placing in their true situations the many dangers, &c., and thereby aiding and benefiting navigation as well as science, &c.

Further, your petitioner and his associates, in their arduous enterprises and persevering endeavours for many years past, to the general national good, and to promote this fishery, and commercial trade, and in discoveries, have had the fortune to discover a new continent, or extensive lands, in the southern hemisphere:—which, by the generous act, as due to American enterprise, of a talented circumnavigator,* belonging to a powerful and magnanimous

* The commander of the Russian Discovery Ships.

nation, has received the name of Palmer's Land, and which, it is earnestly desired, may be explored and surveyed by this prayed-for national expedition, for the general public good of our nation; as it is yet uncertain what valuable sources of rich furs, oils, &c., it may contain and supply to our hardy, adventurous, South Sea mariners.

Now, therefore, your petitioner doth humbly pray, that this much required government expedition be sent out to endeavour to obtain those national benefits herein set forth, and which cannot, as in evidence by trial, be done or performed by any private means.

As your memorialist is of opinion such a national discovery and exploring expedition would, in a very weighty degree, accomplish those before-mentioned benefits to navigation, commerce, the fisheries, science, &c., your petitioner is likewise strongly in the belief, that said expedition, in traversing those unfrequented seas, would make new discoveries of lands and islands, which would likely tend to advance our commercial trade, &c.

Also, further, that they would search out, discover, and mark down at inhabited as well as at uninhabited *lands* and islands, as also at the sea-banks and coral reefs, new depots, sources, &c., where those products could be again procured in abundance, viz. of sandal wood, bird's nest, beach-la-mer, pearls, turtle shell, &c., which would much revive again this commercial trade to China, &c.

Furthermore, your petitioner feels confident that this expedition would discover, and do an act of great humanity in their routes, by falling in with and returning again to their homes, some of those now missing ships' crews of American citizens thus long absent from their country, families, friends, and civil society, and which, perhaps, are now dragging out a lonesome and suffering life, after being cast away upon some uninhabited island, or in slavery to some cannibal chief on an inhabited one; which pains the heart in deep distress of feeling in the suffering thought of those most unfortunate missing fellow-citizens and voyagers:—And, to relieve even a single ship's crew of them by such an expedition, what a parental act of government this! And yet further, your petitioner feels sure that they would greatly benefit and improve navigation by exploration and survey, and in correcting the situations, and placing them true on the charts, to be in use, of many islands and dangers, and thereby make the now dangerous hazard much less to the mariner, in our whale, seal, and trading ships and vessels, when traversing those oceans and seas.

Finally, all will admit that such an expedition would add much to history, science, &c., and your memorialist is sincere in the belief, that, if land is not discovered in the way, they may reach a very high south latitude, if not in the vicinity of the south pole. The noted voyager, Captain Weddell, who obtained to the S. latitude of 74° 15′ states, in this latitude the sea was then free of ice, and that he had fine mild weather. And should the American expedition discover land in their way on proceeding south on its examination, who knows but what it may afford or produce invaluable and rich furs, oils, &c., in addition to a new discovery?

And your petitioner would here respectfully remark, with a view to show the weight and length of time his mind has been engaged intent on this exploring subject, and requests, in all deference, permission to state in illustration, that, while engaged in the command and agency in prosecuting those South Sea, Pacific, and China voyages, he has for upwards of thirty years past, had before his mind's eye the evidences of the advantages and benefits of such an exploring expedition to his nation, with the constant increasing surmises and evidences coming up before him in observation, touching and relating to the most *proper kind of vessels,* with their fitments, &c., to enable and give the most sanguine promise to such an expedition, to obtain the greatest favourable and brilliant result; which, if this petition be granted, he is freely willing to communicate for the national benefit.

Also, personal experience has taught the subscriber that situations will occur on such voyages of exploration, both in high and low latitudes, which would be fatal to the large and heavy ship, when the small and lighter vessel would escape.

The writer of this has wintered in his ship in a high latitude, in the icy region towards the south pole, and personally observed the formation, and make, and movements of the ice islands, bergs, &c., on the break up of the winter, and of its frozen massy barriers, causing a terrific, thundering roar, like that of ten thousand cannon, seemingly making terra-firma tremble to its foundations; and been with his ship in very trying and painful situations, in the mountainous swell of rolling billows or turgid seas, in calms and currents, in the equatorial latitudes among the coral reefs, when at the same time beset and surrounded by the savages, which would have been fatal, beyond the possibility of human means, to extricate her, if a heavy ship, but having a lighter vessel, he escaped from this awaiting dreadful fate; but which happened to be the lot of our first ship, and all on board of her which was sent to the Feejee Islands after sandal wood, &c.:—she being a full built, heavy vessel, was wrecked by drifting, and being hove by the billowed sea, in a calm and current on the coral reef, and every soul on board of her, save the Tonga native pilot, perished, or were massacred by the savages, as each individual obtained, through the breakers and surf, a foothold on the rocks

A similar situation and case was no doubt the fate and destruction of the much-lamented and unfortunate La Perouse, his frigates and their crews, which, with more proper and lighter vessels, would perhaps have been avoided.

Also, as an additional evidence of weight of advantage such an exploring has been to his mind, he would respectfully mention a fact, viz.: That an expedition of two ships was prepared, and nearly ready for sea in their departure on this service, in the spring of 1812, under his command, and a commission was granted by the President of the United States, to your petitioner, in the command of the same, when the sudden declaration of war by Congress put a stop to its sailing, and finally caused it to be abandoned.

Your petitioner also respectfully begs, it will be here noted, that since that date the additional weighty call, or necessity, that such a national expedition should be sent out, is, that the important discovery of the continent of *Palmer's Land* has been made by Americans; which will also show in evidence, that in our South Sea mariners' and voyagers' minds, at least, this exploring project petitioned for is not a visionary idea, but for real and important national benefits that are much needed.

All which is most respectfully submitted.

EDMUND FANNING.

December 7th, 1833.

Notes explanatory of the subject of the National Exploring Expedition, or,—A plain tale of facts, &c.

Thus is recorded the official memorial of evidence of the acts, and doings of a citizen, whom the Almighty, in his goodness, has been pleased to bless with a long life of three score and ten; nearly fifty years of which having been spent in the enterprise of voyaging in research and discovery tending greatly to the benefit of his country and its citizens, as well as the pecuniary benefits, he trusts, that a just and liberal public will not suffer now to be taken from him in the hoar age of life, the small award due to any merit he may be deserving of,—while he, in the best of feelings, does not wish and is not desirous of taking from any fellow-being the least feather's weight of the credit due to them, in recording those historical facts which he conceives in justice belong to himself and those of name dear to him.

Sundry prints have, with many flattering puffs, given the whole credit and merit as projector and procurer of the authorization by Congress of the American South Sea Exploring Expedition, to *another citizen*, who truly and richly is entitled and deserving of a large share of merit in this national measure. But the author of this work would respectfully ask to here note the following explanations corroborated by facts, vouchers, &c., in addition to a reference to those extracts of memorials, in vindication of just credit to his doings, and acts relative to, or touching on the measure of sending out this laudable national enterprise, viz.

This citizen, to whom those prints give all credit, sailed in 1829, from the United States; as one of the scientific corps in the American Exploring Brigs, Seraph and Annawan, sent out under the directive agency of the author of this volume; and he did not return to the United States until the Frigate Potomac, Commodore Downes, in May, 1834. This being the fact, and referring to the foregoing extracts of memorials, how can his friends, those editors, claim for him the merit of being the first projector of this expedition, and moreover of procuring its authorization by Congress, when the measure had, at his return, been thus already urged by the author of this work with unwearied zeal, before that honourable body for three sessions, and the honourable senators, and members, it is presumed, had now become familiar with the project, as also to have an earnest patriotic interest in the fair promise of the honour and benefit such an enterprise would be to the nation. The extracts of the memorials and proceedings can be corroborated by a reference to the records of Congress, as also by hundreds of most respectable citizens (solicited by him) who supported the author's petition to Congress by their memorials.

Farther, as the earliest in bringing this exploring subject before government, see Fanning's Voyages, page 492, where it will appear in evidence, that the author had the honour to bring this subject before government, in 1810 and 12, during Mr. Madison's presidency. The author, therefore, freely leaves it with his fellow-citizens, and the respective readers, to decide to whom belongs the merit of projector, &c., if there be any beyond that to which every patriotic citizen may be entitled.

He will only in all due deference add, that at the time of the arrival of the Potomac, it was well known that the project was advancing in Congress, in a sure prospect of its authorization; and any citizen being single, without a family to support, could as well board himself in Washington City, as at any other place, during the sessions,—and could put in a petition to Congress, for any project he pleased, even if the same had already been petitioned for; and at same time, by thus forming a numerous acquaintance, and more especially when possessing shining elemental advantages of education, embellished by address, he could, by the aid of high literary acquirements, orations, &c., cause an impression on the public mind and press to go forth, that he was the sole projector, &c., of such a measure. To correct which in this case, the author conceived it due in justice, disclaiming all intentional censure or disrespect, to here respectfully note these explanations, &c., without the most remote desire, or intention to hurt the feelings, or to take from any active, and patriotic citizen, one iota of his claim of merit. But only to explain and lay the case fairly and plainly before the public, that the real *Simon Pure* may have his just proportion of the award, if there be any other than ordinary. At the time of the authorization of this expedition by Congress, its fair bill was before the House of Representatives, and when, in its turn, it should have been taken up, would undoubtedly then have passed, and it is believed by a greater majority, and in a better conciliating satisfaction, than on the course it went through, in the general appropriation bill. However, the honourable Senator, S. L. Southard, thought proper, with what view he best knows, to move in the honourable United States' Senate, the authorization for this measure of a sloop of war, etc., in the general naval appropriation bill—whereupon it passed. Now, if the honourable senator made this move with the view to secure the president's sanction, it was perfectly needless—as might have been known by one word with the venerable president on the subject; as the author was present at Washington, at the time urging forward the project, and from his oral communication with the Executive, to his certain knowledge, he is decidedly in the belief, that our venerable, patriotic president, would as willingly and cheerfully, and that in earnest zealous support, have then signed the fair bill on its passage, as that of any other bill whatever, that was signed by him during his presidency; and what relatively follows hereafter in this volume, will, it is presumed, show to the satisfactory corroboration of this fact.

The Peacock attempt.—The public, it is presumed, are well informed of the attempt, by the re-building and preparation of the sloop of war, Peacock, to fit out an exploring expedition to the South Seas, during the years 1827–8, under the presidency of the Hon. J. Q. Adams, by the authority of a resolution of the honourable House of Representatives of the United States only; and its failure and abandonment, on the change of the next presidency and administration under General Andrew Jackson—leaving an unfavourable impression on the minds of President Jackson and his executive counsellors, towards such a project—owing, no doubt, to the absence of correct information, by or from experienced explanations on the subject, relative to its needy importance to the nation, as also to the national benefits it would be to commerce, the whale and seal fisheries, navigation, science, &c., &c., as well as to the honour of the nation and its gallant navy. This unfavourable impression absolutely required to be removed, and a contra-favourable impression made and established, before any hope could be had of a bill being passed by Congress and ratified by the President, authorizing such a South Sea discovery and exploring expedition. This the author zealously undertook, and the following vouchers and evidences will, with the sequel, show how well and happily he succeeded.

On repairing to Washington, at the commencement of the session of Congress, in 1831, with the petition to present to Congress for such a national measure, he was accompanied by two able and well-informed citizens, to aid in his explanations and to remove the difficulty, and bring about, if possible, a favourable opinion and result, as well as to raise up a determination in the government to carry the enterprise into effect.

The following proceedings took place, as related in the letter of the author, (herewith,) to President Van Buren.

From the files of a mass of voluminous correspondence by the author, had during his persevering, industrious aid, to effect this South Sea exploring expedition, the following letters, extracts, &c., are hereby submitted, as evidence of his acts and doings in favour and support of this laudable national project.

On the close of General Jackson's presidency, and soon after President Van Buren's administration had commenced, doubts were mentioned as to this expedition ever being sent out. Therefore, to aid in *its sure sailing*, the author addressed a letter of explanation, &c., to the Executive on the subject, of which the following is an *extract*.

New-York, June 12th, 1837.

To His Excellency Martin Van Buren, P esident of the United States, Washington City.

I respectfully request to place before the President, the following further information, &c., viz :—

Before presenting the petition to Congress on this subject of a National South Sea Exploring expedition, early in December, 1831, I, with an experienced commander in explorations in the southern hemisphere,* and also a

* Captain Benjamin Pendleton, senior in the command, and John Frampton Watson, Esq., M.D., Professor, and of the scientific corps of the American Exploring Expedition

scientific citizen of first qualification, who had also voyaged to that part of our globe, waited on President Jackson, explained our views of its merits, and the honour, benefits, &c., which would likely result to the nation by a government discovery and exploring expedition to the South Seas, &c.,—The President listened attentively, in much interest;—and in conclusion observed, he saw its merits, and the benefits that might be obtained to our commerce, the fisheries, navigation, &c., &c.,—said we could present the petition, and if Congress would authorize the project, it should now have his ready and earnest support, desiring me, on taking leave, to give my views, &c., on the subject to the secretary of the navy. Accordingly we the next morning waited on, at his department, the Honourable Secretary Woodbury, submitted to him our views, &c., (that able and highly worthy officer, Commodore Rogers, being present,) when Mr. Woodbury requested, firstly,—the perusal of our petition to Congress, then, in his usual patriotism, observed, like the President, if Congress should authorize the measure, it should receive his ready support.

of brigs Seraph and Annawan, which had been sent out to those seas, patronized by the executive government of the United States.

This gave encouragement to present the petition, as also my attendance, session after session, zealously urging forward the project, up to its authorization.

Having the honor to be
With high regard,
The President's obdt. servt.
EDMUND FANNING.

Copy of a letter from the Honourable Secretary of the navy, to the author.

Navy Department, December 7, 1832.

Sir,—Your letter of the 5th instant (on the exploring expedition) has been received. I will be very happy to carry into execution any directions Congress may be pleased to give, on the interesting subject of your letter.

I am respectfully, sir, your ob'd't servant,
LEVI WOODBURY.

Captain EDMUND FANNING,
New-York.

Extracts from the letters to the author from the honourable G. C. Verplanck, of the House of Representatives; and the honourable Senator Robbins, of the United States' Senate; and from the honourable secretary of the navy, of date, Navy Department, 15th June 1836, *will show in evidence*, the opinion of the government relative to the part, and interest in aid the author had taken and performed to the authorization, &c., of this National South Sea Discovery and Exploring Expedition project, with likewise that of his ability relative to the important command of it.

Washington, February 9, 1831.

Dear Sir,—Your communications on the subject of the National Discovery Expedition have been duly received. The expedition of discovery cannot but prove a valuable addition to geographical and commercial knowledge, to which I shall be happy to contribute any aid or advice in my power,

I am, with respect, your ob'd't servant,

G. C. VERPLANK.

Captain E. FANNING,
New-York.

Washington City, February 13, 1833.

Dear Sir,—I have received your letter of the 11th inst. I view the project (of a National South Sea Exploring Expedition) suggested, as you do, as one of great national importance.

With great respect, your ob'd't servant,

ASHER ROBBINS.

Captain EDMUND FANNING,
New-York.

Navy Department, 15th June 1836.

If Congress had authorized such Exploring Expedition to be conducted by citizens and not by officers of the navy, your claim to command the expedition would be a strong one,—but Congress have made it an affair of the navy,—and I find you renounce all desire to sail in the expedition, as you believe the officers of the navy equal in all respects to the task.

Your zeal in procuring a law for an explorer's expedition is well known.

I am, with great respect, your ob'd't servant,

M. DICKERSON.

Captain E. FANNING,
New-York.

And as further evidence that the author continued to the latest to contribute his humble aid to the expedition, he would here respectfully remark, that, having received assurance from the honourable secretary of the navy, that any suggestions relative to the choice of route to be taken by the expedition, after sailing from the port of the United States, would be very acceptable, whereby the author promptly tendered the following herein after mentioned four pages of suggestions, &c., which were forwarded by mail, enclosed in his letter, as per copy herewith.

(COPY.)

New-York, September 6th, 1837.

Dear Sir,—Agreeable to your favour of the 29th ult., I have the honour herewith to forward the enclosed views on route, &c.

With great respect, your ob'd't servant.

E. FANNING.

To the Hon. Mahlon Dickerson,
Secretary U. States' Navy,
Washington City.

Note.—The enclosed paper in this letter to the honourable secretary of the navy, contained four pages closely written of the author's extensive views, suggestions, &c., relative to the most promising route for the expedition to take on its departing from our port, and on navigating in the South Seas, &c. Likewise informing of the most convenient harbours, and places of rendezvous, &c. &c.

The following is a copy of the letter from the

honourable secretary of the navy, acknowledging the receipt of the same.

(COPY.)

Navy Department, September 8th, 1837.

Sir,—I have received your letter of the 6th inst., with your suggestions as to the route for the S. S. Exploring Expedition,—for which I thank you. They shall receive a respectful consideration.

I am with great respect, your ob'd't servant,

M. DICKERSON.

Captain EDMUND FANNING.

Copy of a letter from Commodore Chauncey, to the Honourable Noyes Barber, member of the United States' Congress.

Navy Commissioners' Office,
February 22d, 1834.

Dear Sir,—I have the pleasure to receive your favour of the 19th inst., enclosing a communication from E. Fanning, Esq., upon the subject of an Exploring Expedition to the South Seas, etc. I have known Captain Fanning since I was a boy, and believe him to be as pure and disinterested a patriot as any in our country, and I am persuaded that he has no interested* motive in recommending to Congress the adoption of some measure to explore the southern oceans.

I am, dear sir, very truly yours,

J. CHAUNCEY.

Hon. NOYES BARBER, M. C.
House of Representatives,
Washington City.

If the general reader please, it may be noticed that the dates to the small number of vouchers here inserted, are sufficient to show the chain of constant attention of the author to the subject of this Exploring Expedition, from the Session of Congress in 1831, the time of the presentation of his petition, up to and after its authorization by Congress, and to the time of its near sailing, by his *offers of aid* to its routes. Nevertheless, having reason to conceive, now the expedition is authorized, and fearing that the author's name should be omitted, with his *small* proportion of merit, (by active movements with the purest desire to serve his country,) in the volume of the voyage,

* A report had, at this time, got circulated, that the author was exerting himself to obtain the authorization of this expedition, with a view to self employ.

at the return of this National South Sea Expedition, he has deemed it but justice, to here respectfully insert these explanations and vouchers.* After so many years of voluntary, but zealous struggling, together with much pecuniary sacrifice, and time spent in attendance on Congress, travelling, etc., by the author; he feels reluctant, now that the object is obtained, and the expedition duly authorized, to be thus put aside into oblivion, like a worn out cipher; and therefore feels that a generous public will excuse and indulge him in thus placing the sub-

* See Army and Navy Chronicle for December 1st, 1836, where the Honourable Secretary of the Navy, in his letter of date, Navy Department, September 12th, 1836, to Captain Jones, the senior officer in command of this expedition, has this paragraph:

"The person with whom you intimate I have corresponded, I presume, is Captain Edmund Fanning, of New-York.

"Captain Fanning long since planned a South Sea Exploring Expedition, and has been urging it upon Congress ever since the administration of Mr Madison. So far as there is a merit in suggesting and urging this measure, it is due to Captain Fanning. He is intimately acquainted with many regions which it is intended to explore; and it is very desirable to have the benefit of his knowledge and experience, both in fitting out and conducting the expedition.

"I am, very respectfully, your obedient servant,

"M. DICKERSON."

"Captain THOMAS AP. C. JONES,
U. S. Navy."

ject in its true light before them. With all due respect, he thinks that the handsome invitation* (declined) given to him by the honourable secretary of the U. S. Navy, to go out in the expedition, will put at rest any thought of his ever having acted (as has been remarked) with a view to self-interest, of future employment and emolument, but solely for the good of his country, and the inhabitants on other parts of the face of our globe. This is the real state of the case.

The author would here with respectful deference, remark, that the vessels that now compose the Exploring Expedition, (except the frigate and her store-ship,†) are not such as would by him have been preferred or selected.‡

* His reason for declining will satisfactorily appear in the publication of the author's life and correspondence, viz.—his being so far advanced in the time of life given to the age of man.

† The author would much prefer a properly constructed single ship to even these two, for this special service, to act as the Flag ship.

‡ During the year 1811, that able and talented shipwright, Henry Eckford, built for the author two ships of about 330 tons each, on the most approved model, as was supposed, for this special service of discovery and exploring vessels. On trial these proved to be first rate buoyant sea boats, and very swift sailing, and alert working vessels. On finishing them, this very ingenious builder plainly showed, that by a different plan in the construction from the usual mode;—of

They will undoubtledly answer the purpose to a certain degree, but, those far better adapted might have been procured, which would have insured a promise of the utmost degree of comfort, safety, and despatch. Having had ves-

mechanical improvement in their support and security, by clamp framed decks, and chain braced frames, (which system of plan, on explanation, is not only convincingly more efficient, and far superior, but would readily appear as simple, when explained, as was that of the greatest discoverer Columbus, in making the egg stand on its end,) in the like models as were the above two vessels; that there could be procured for this exploring service, two of similar model and construction, which would be far superior in performance, comfort, and safety in heavy weather, or among dangers by ice &c., as also for swift sailing, and alert working, it is believed, to what has ever yet been produced by any nation. The long experience the author has had in navigating in every clime, was, by this evidence confirmable in his mind as most superior, and would no doubt be decidedly and highly approved of by the first judges as preferable; as surely giving to their commanders the means and aid of doing and performing far beyond, and in much greater safety and despatch, than what as yet ever has been done or performed by man. Such as these are the kind of vessels which the author was so very anxious his country should have the advantage of for explorers in this first American National Exploring Expedition, in the room of those heavily, clumsily built, old fashioned brigs and schooners, now attached for this part of the service. Further, with two such exploring vessels, on the Eckford plan, the expedition would have been, Fulton-like, new, and truly American.

sels built for this service in the earliest of all adventures on the briny ocean, or icy seas, by one of the first shipwrights that ever took draft or model in hand, (the lamented Eckford,) and being only zealously anxious that this first American national trial, should have in its service the best adapted vessels which would give the fairest promise to excel; and because the author's practical experience could not admit that the Pioneer, Consort, and Pilot,* were the best adapted vessels for this service that could be procured, it has been ungenerously reported, that he was opposed to the expedition. Opposed to it, indeed!—when our globe revolves to the west, and not to the east, then, and not till then, will this be the fact. How illiberally unjust! And after the author's long untiring task of zealous attention, and urging to obtain the authorization and fit out of this first national Exploring Expedition; he cannot but respectfully remark, that it has not, even now, such an important and magnificent na-

* This vessel, it is already said, has been condemned, as unfit for the service she was built for, and put at rest to remain in port as a receiving ship. This being the fact, can there be a stronger evidence of the want of deficiency of experienced information and knowledge in the preparations, construction of the proper vessels, &c., in the fit out of this expedition?

tional enterprise been managed and prepared, as the author's experience would have counselled ; and yet, its expenditure has been altogether unprecedented. His tendered knowledge, and long experience, when communicated, have been mainly put aside and unlistened to, in its fit out. It is presumed, however, that its able commander will hereafter have the gallant generosity to explain why this has so been; at least, it is thought judicious to thus leave this circumstance, until the result of the expedition is known. Nevertheless, as the real facts are, as herein penned, and so plainly related, and substantially supported, relative to his acts, and doings, in the aid to its authorization,—may it not be respectfully asked, is not every citizen in the expedition, from its talented commander, down to the smallest boy, under, at least, some small obligation to the author, for their desired station in the voyage? But time will show, whether the gallant officer appointed to this very honourable, brilliant, and important command, of one of the noblest, and highest stations to commendable ambitious pride, will cause justice to be given on the volume of the records of the voyage to an unaspiring citizen, (the author,) or leave it, as a vacant spot, or tarnished mark, on the bright and shining escutcheon of this laudable national enterprise. He has only to add, (if it ever sails,) that whatever the event, or result of the expedition may be, it now has the most ardent wish of the author, that it will be brilliantly fortunate, and terminate in additional fresh honour, glory, and benefit to the American name, nation, and navy ; as also to those patriotic adventurers who sail in it.

Finally, with the utmost respect be it said, it is as sure, as that the sun shines at noon, in a clear day, that this American National South Sea Exploring Expedition, would *not*, now, (in October 1837,) have been authorized, had not the author of this work been in being, and a citizen of these United States,* this is the absolute fact, whatever its result may turn out to be. Therefore, for future proof, this passage is here recorded ; because, not any other citizen, it is presumed, could have hoped to, or so successfully and happily have explained away the

* And yet, with all deference, the plan and proceedings of its fit out, are so wide from the author's views, that with such exploring vessels as the provided brigs and schooners are, it brings fears, that, after all, it may result in no great benefit, &c., to the nation, if it do not prove in the end, better if it never had been authorized. This would be truly discouraging to American patriotic enterprise,—which may the Giver of all good prevent. However, what is herein related will be an historical record of its rise and progress—let its result be what it may.

wrong or unfavourable impression, on the mind of the President, to such a national project; and made it appear thus greatly to the honour and benefit of the nation, except he had had the like personal experience as the author, who also had the fortune to hold, and was favoured in weight of argument, by that of the honour of holding a commission (*which was submitted*) in the command of a similar Discovery and Exploring Expedition, granted to the author by President Madison, a former Executive of the United States, highly eminent in the rank of wisdom as a statesman. For what avail would it have been, even for Congress to have passed a bill authorizing it, if the unfavourable impression had not been first removed, as the President, it is well known, possessed the power of veto.

In order to show the public, and general reader, that there has been no holding back of aid, or neglect on the part of the author, in ever promptly giving his assistance to this national enterprise; he would state, in farther illustration and explanation, that previous to any appointment whatever being made to this American National South Sea Exploring Expedition, the author tendered his services in aid of superintending the preparations, construction of the proper vessels, &c., in its out fit; this was done by a letter to his Excellency the President of the United States, forwarded under cover to a patriotic and prominent Hon Member of Congress, who was well acquainted with the author's long and arduous perseverance in the obtaining its authorization, with the request that he would have the kindness to pass it in person into the hand of the President. The author, in due time, received a line from this gentleman, (the honourable Richard M. Johnson,) stating that he had handed the letter of tender to the President, who received it, in thankful kindness, and said it should receive a respectful consideration. Soon after, the author received a letter from the honourable Secretary of the United States' Navy, remarking that the author's letter to the President, tendering his services in aid of the fit out of the Exploring Expedition, had been referred to his department, and when the time arrived for taking up, and acting on the subject, it should have the most respectful consideration.* Here

* The decline, or objection to the aid of the author, who possessed much experience relating to the subject of the preparation, construction of the proper vessels, &c., for the expedition, could not have rested with His Excellency, the President, or Hon. Secretary of the Navy. For the reasons of this opinion, see the extract of letter, from Army and Navy Chronicle for December 1st, 1836. Page 128.

the author's tender of assistance has rested, and since remained in silence; but why it has thus, silently remained, and why his long personal practice, experience, and information on the subject, has been put aside, he has not the means of explaining. Subsequently an extensive correspondence with the honourable Secretary of the Navy, has taken place on the project, concerning information, &c., which information, the author, notwithstanding, has been ever ready to contribute, but which, in the main, has had very little useful effect. For what reason it has so been, the author is left in the dark.

A list of the vessels, officers, and scientific corps, which compose the American National South Sea Exploring Expedition. The following being a correct list, as reported, at this date, of the United States' South Sea Exploring Expedition, November 20, 1837.*

* Since the date of this list, by the tenor of a letter, the author has subsequently received on the subject, from the Hon. Secretary of the Navy, it appears, that alterations of stations and officers, may yet take place before the expedition sails.

The Flag Ship, U. S. Frigate, Macedonian.

Commodore Thomas Ap Catesby Jones, senior in command.

Captain James Armstrong.

Lieutenants George A. Magruder, Andrew K. Long, Arthur Sinclair, and Thomas Turner.

Acting Master, H. J. Hartstone.

Fleet Surgeon, B. Tickner. Assistants, John L. Fox, and J. J. Abernethy.

Commodore's Secretary, William M. Stewart.

Passed Midshipmen, J. A. Underwood, and W. S. Swan.

Midshipmen, Samuel Smith, Catesby Ap R. Jones, James L. Blair, Archibald M'Rae, Daniel Ammen, J. C. Wait, D. Williamson, F. A. Parker, H. H. Harrison.

Commodore's Clerk, J. S. Nevins.

Captain's Clerk, G. A. Thomas.

Boatswain, John Shannon.

Gunner, Gustavus Newman.

Carpenter, L. R. Townsend.

Sail Maker, Samuel B. Banister.

Purser, William Speiden.

Purser's Steward, Franklin Curtis.

Officer of Marines, Commanding, Captain James Eledin.

New Store Ship, The Relief.

Lieutenant Commandant, Thomas A. Dornan.

Lieutenant, Stephen C. Rowan.

Acting Master, R. F. Pinkney.

Passed Midshipmen, J. H. North, W. L. Maury, and George T. Sinclair.

Assistant Surgeon, E. Gilchrist.

Captain's Clerk J. Howison.

Boatswain, W. Black.

Gunner, A. A. Peterson.
Carpenter, W. S. Laighton.
Sail Maker, S. V. Hawkins.
Purser's Clerk, J. S. Barnard.

New Brig, Pioneer.

Lieutenant Commandant, William D. Newman.
Lieutenant, Samuel P. Lee.
Acting Master, M. G. L. Clairbone.
Passed Midshipmen, E. T. Shubrick, William Postell, and R. J. P. Sandford.
Boatswain, George Wilmouth.
Carpenter, Amos Chicks.
Gunner, Oliver Nelson.
Purser's Clerk, W. M. Clerk.

New Brig, Consort.

Lieutenant Commandant, James Glyna.
Passed Midshipman, George M. Totten.
Acting Master, B. M. Dove.
Assistant Surgeon, C. Gullion.
Boatswain, H. Welton.
Gunner, J. D. Anderson.
Carpenter, John Fry.
Sail Maker, J. Joines.
Purser's Clerk, R. H. Griffin.

*New Schooner, Pilot.**

Lieutenant Commandant, Mannings, Commander.

* This reported condemned, as inadequate for this service, and left at Baltimore as a receiving vessel.†

† The author would not be understood by any thing said in this volume, as casting any reflections, or making any personal complaint

Schooner Active.

Lieutenant W. W. Woolsey, Commander.

Corresponding Secretary to the Expedition, J. N. Reynolds, Esq.

Historiographer to the Expedition, the Rev. Walter Colter.

Astronomer to the Expedition, Professor E. C. Ward, Esq.

Scientific Corps.

A. Grey, Esq., M.D. New-York.
R. Hoyle, Esq., do.
A. Agate, Esq., do.
J. Eights, Esq., M.D. Albany.
C. Pickering, Esq., M.D. Philadelphia.
R. Coates, Esq., M. D. do.
T. R. Peale, Esq., do.
W. R. Johnson, Esq., do.
E. H. Darley, Esq., do.
J. Drayton, Esq., do.
J. W. Randal, Esq., Boston.
J. P. Couthony, Esq., do.
H. E. Hale, Esq., do.
J. L. Dand, Esq., New-Haven.
W. Rich, Esq., Washington, D. C.

Containing in the Expedition, six hundred and twenty-one persons, including the Scientific Corps and their assistants.*

whatever. But he cannot refrain from here respectfully mentioning his utmost regret, that it has been judged advisable *not* to accept and use his experienced knowledge to the benefit of the nation, and the expedition, in the construction of its vessels, and aid in outfits. As to what would be the most promising fitments, in its fit out, in warranting the greatest and most brilliant result to such an expedition, have been in its occasional collections weighty on his mind, for upwards of thirty years past.

* See Appendix.

NOTE.—From the Annual Report of the Honourable Mahlon Dickerson, Secretary of the United States' Navy, to His Excellency the President of the United States, of date, Navy Department, 2d of December, 1837, wherein he thus remarks:—That the Board of Commissioners (consisting of those very able and talented officers, Commodores Chauncey, Morris, Warrington, Patterson, and Wadsworth, who had been ordered on a survey of examination of the exploring vessels,) state, that had they "been called upon before any preparations had been made, to state the number and character of the vessels, which, in their opinion, would be best calculated to secure the attainment of these proposed objects, they certainly would *not* have recommended those which have been prepared," viz. the Pioneer, Consort, and Pilot.

PART VI.

A DESCRIPTION OF THE NEW SOUTH SHETLAND ISLES, BY JAMES EIGHTS, ESQ., M.D., NATURALIST IN THE SCIENTIFIC CORPS IN THE AMERICAN EXPLORING EXPEDITION, OF BRIGS SERAPH AND ANNAWAN UNDER THE COMMAND OF CAPTAIN B. PENDLETON, AND N. B. PALMER, SENT OUT TO THE SOUTH SEAS UNDER THE DIRECTIVE AGENCY OF THE AUTHOR OF THIS WORK, AND THE PATRONAGE OF GOVERNMENT IN THE YEARS 1829 and 1830.

Location of the Islands—Snowy elevation—Straits and bays—Beautiful clearness of the atmosphere—Icebergs—Penguin assemblages—Antarctic sky—Brilliant hue and reflections — Whale skeletons — Geological features—Craggy eminences—Singular ebb and flow of the tide—Current along the coast—The strata and minerals—Volcanoes—Animals—Mermaid—Sea skunks—Birds—King penguins and its eggs—Rookery penguins—Existence of a southern continent—Palmer's Land.

THE new South Shetland Isles are situated between 61° and 63° south latitude, and 54° and 63° west longitude. They are formed by an extensive cluster of rocks rising abruptly from the ocean, to a considerable height above its surface. Their true elevation cannot be easily determined, in consequence of the heavy masses of snow which lie over them, concealing them almost entirely from the sight. Some of them, however, rear their glistening summits, to an altitude of about three thousand feet, and when the heavens are free from clouds, imprint a sharp and well defined outline upon the intense blueness of the sky. They are divided every where by straits, and indented by deep bays, or coves: many of which afford to vessels a comfortable shelter from the rude gales to which these high latitudes are so subject. When the winds have ceased to blow, and the ocean is at rest, nothing can exceed the beautiful clearness of the atmosphere in these elevated regions. The numerous furrows and ravines which every where impress the snowy acclivity of the hills, are distinctly visible for fifty or sixty miles; and the various sea-fowl, resting upon the slight eminences, and brought in strong relief against the sky, ofttimes deceive the experienced eye of the mariner, by having their puny dimensions magnified in size to those of human form.

The ocean in the vicinity, so far as the eye has vision, is here and there studded with icebergs, varying in magnitude from a few feet to more than a mile in extent, and not unfrequently rising two hundred feet in the air, presenting every variety of form, from the snug white-washed cottage of the peasant, to the enormous architectural piles, containing either broadly expanded Grecian domes, or having the many lofty and finely attenuated spires of some Gothic structure.

The sun, even at midsummer, attains but a moderate altitude in these dreary regions, and when its horizontal beams illumine these masses of ice, their numerous angles and indentations, catching the light as they move along, exhibit all the beautiful gradations of colour, from an emerald green, to that of the finest blue. Some of them, whose sloping sides will admit of their ascent, are tenanted by large assemblies of Penguins, whose chattering noise may be heard on a still day at an incredible distance over the clear smooth surface of the sea.

When the storms rage and the ocean rolls its mountain wave against their slippery sides, the scene is truly sublime. Tall columns of spray shooting up far above their tops, soon become dissipated in clouds of misty white ; gradually descending, they envelop the whole mass for a short time, giving to it much the appearance of being covered with a veil of silvery gauze. When thus agitated, they not unfrequently explode with the noise of thunder, scattering their fragments far and wide over the surrounding surface of the deep. These hills of ice are borne onwards at a considerable rate by the wind and the velocity of the current—when so, they sweep along with a majesty that nothing else can equal.

The sky, too, in these latitudes, presents a very singular aspect; being, most generally filled with innumerable clouds, torn into ragged and irregular patches by the wild gales which every where race over the Antarctic Seas: the sun, as it rises or sets slowly and obliquely in the northern horizon, sends its rays through the many openings between, tinging them here and there with every variety of hue and colour, from whence they are thrown in mild and beautiful reflection upon the extensive fields of snow which lie piled on the surrounding hills, giving to the whole scene for a greater part of the long summer day, the ever-varying effect of a most gorgeous sunset.

Although many of the scenes about these islands are highly exciting, the effect produced on the mind, by their general aspect, is cold and cheerless to an unusual degree, for on their lonely shores the voice of man is seldom heard; the only indication of his ever having trod the soil, is the solitary grave of some poor seaman near the beach, and the only wood that any where meets the eye, are the staves that mark its dimensions ; no sound for years disturb the silence of the scene, save the wild screech of the sea-birds as they wing their way in search of their accustomed food—the incessant chattering of the congregated penguins—the rude blasts, tearing among the icy hills—the sullen roar of the waves, tumbling and dashing along the shores, or the heavy explosions of the large masses of snow falling into the waves beneath, to form the vast icebergs which every where drift through the southern ocean. The shores of these islands are generally formed by the perpendicular cliffs of ice, frequently reaching for many miles, and rising from ten feet to several hundred in height. In many places at their base, the continued action of the water has worn out deep caves with broadly arched roofs, under which the ocean rolls its waves with a subterranean sound that strikes most singularly on the ear, and when sufficiently undermined, extensive portions crack off with an astounding report, creating a tremendous surge in the sea below, which, as it rolls over its surface, sweeps every thing before it, from the smallest animal that feeds upon its bottom, to those of the greatest bulk.

Entire skeletons of the whale, fifty or sixty feet in length, are not unfrequently found in elevated situations along the shores, many feet above high water line, and I know of no other cause capable of producing this effect. Whales are very common in this vicinity, and in calm weather great numbers of them may be seen breaking the surface of the ocean in the many intervals which occur between the numerous icebergs, sometimes sending forth volumes of spray, at others elevating their huge flukes in the air to descend head first, as it were, to fathom the ocean's depth. When they perish, either from accident or some natural cause, their carcasses, in drifting towards the shore, are overtaken by the billows and thrown thus far upon land. Here they are left by the retiring wave, and in a few hours their bones become perfectly denuded by the numberless sea-birds that feed upon the flesh.

The geological features that these islands present in these high favoured situations, where the continuous power of the winds has swept bare the rocks, correspond in a great measure with their desolate and dreary aspect. They are composed principally of vertical columns of basalt, resting upon the strata of argillaceous conglomerate; the pillars are united in detached groups, having at their bases sloping banks constructed of materials which are constantly accumulating by fragments from above.

These groups rise abruptly from the irregularly elevated plains, over whose surface they are scattered here and there, presenting an appearance to the eye not unlike some old castle crumbling into ruin, and when situated upon the sand stone promontories that occasionally jut out into the sea, they tower aloft in solitary grandeur over its foaming waves; sometimes they may be seen piercing the superincumbent snow, powerfully contrasting their deep murky hues with its spotless purity. Ponds of fresh water are now and then found on the plains, but they do not owe their origin to springs, being formed by the melting of the snow.

The rocky shores of these islands are formed by bold craggy eminences standing out into the sea at different distances from each other, from whose bases dangerous reefs not unfrequently lie out for several miles in extent, rendering it necessary for navigators to keep a cautious watch, after making any part of this coast; the intervals between these crags are composed of narrow strips of plain, constructed of coarsely angulated fragments of every variety of size, which at some previous period have fallen from the surrounding hills. They slope gradually down to the water, terminating in a fine sandy beach. A few rounded pieces of granite are occasionally to be seen lying about, brought unquestionably by the icebergs from their parent hills on some more southern land, as we saw no rocks of this nature, *in situ*, on these islands. In one instance, I obtained a boulder nearly a foot in diameter from one of these floating hills of ice. The action of the waves has produced little or no effect upon the basalt along the coast, as its angles retain all the acuteness of a recent fracture, but when the conglomerate predominates, the mass is generally rounded. The ocean about these shores is generally of great depth; the materials which constitute its bottom are finely comminuted particles, having their origin from the decomposition of the neighbouring rocks. Our stay at these islands occupied a period of four weeks, during which time we observed but one ebb and flow of the tide in twenty four hours. I know not if this be universal, but have been informed by mariners familiar in these seas, that they have generally found it so; if it should prove to be the case, it is a very singular phenomenon. Not a day occurred that snow did not fall or ice make on our decks, and during the time we spent between the latitudes of 60° and 70° south, and 54° and 101° west longitude, which was more than two months, we found the current setting with considerable velocity from the south-west to the north-east. The prevailing winds were also westerly, most commonly from the south-west and north-west.

The colour of the basalt is generally of a greenish black. The prisms are from four to nine sided; most commonly, however, of but six, and from three to four feet in diameter; their greatest length, in an upright position above the subjacent conglomerate, is about eighty feet. Their external surfaces are closely applied to each other, though but slightly united, consequently they are continually falling out by the expansive power of the congealing water among its fissures. When they are exposed to the influence of the atmosphere, for any length of time, they are, for a small depth, of a rusty brown colour, owing, no doubt, to the iron which they contain becoming partially oxydized: sometimes they are covered by a thin coat of quartz and chalcedony.

Clusters of these columns are occasionally seen reposing on their sides, in such a manner as to exhibit the surfaces of the urbases distinctly, which is rough and vesicular. When this is the case they are generally bent, forming quite an arch with the horizon. When they approach the conglomerate for ten or twelve feet, they lose their columnar structure and assume the appearance of a dark-coloured, flinty slate, breaking readily into irregular rhombic fragments: this fine variety, in descending, gradually changes to a greenish colour, and a much coarser structure, until it passes into a most perfect amygdaloid, the cavities being chiefly filled with quartz, amethyst, and chalcedony. Sometimes an interval of about forty or fifty feet occurs between the columns, which space is occupied by the amorphous variety, elevated to some considerable height against them; their edges, in this case, are not at all changed by the contact.

The basalt is very tough and hard; the effect produced upon it by the action of the file is very slight; the steel elicits no sparks; the fragments are angular, with an imperfect conchoidal fracture; its structure is coarsely granular and uneven, and is composed, essentially, of hornblende, felspar, and a greenish substance in grains, much resembling epidote. Crystals of leucite, of a yellow and reddish tinge, are disseminated throughout the mass, whose fractured surfaces strongly reflect the rays of light to the eye; in some places it sensibly affects the needle, owing to its iron. Veins of quartz frequently traverse the fine variety,—some of them containing beautiful amethysts.

The basis rock of these islands, as far as I could discover, is the conglomerate, which underlies the basalt. It is composed, most generally, of two or three layers, about five feet in thickness each, resting one on the other, and dipping to the south-east at an angle of from twelve to twenty degrees.

These layers are divided by regular fissures into large rhombic tables, many of which appear to have recently fallen out, and now lie scattered all over the sloping sides of the hills, so that the strata, when seen cropping out from beneath the basalt, presents a slightly arched row of angular projections of some considerable magnitude and extent.

These strata are chiefly composed of irregular and angular fragments of a rock, whose principal ingredient appears to be green earth, arranged with both a granular and slatey structure, united by argillaceous cement; the whole mass, when moistened by the breath, giving out a strong odour of that earth.

The upper portion of this conglomerate, for a few feet, is of a dirty green colour, and appears to be constructed by the passage of the amygdaloid in this rock, the greenish fragments predominating; and they are united to each other principally by zeolite, of a beautiful light red or orange colour, together with some quartz and chalcedony; a few crystals of lime cause it to effervesce slightly in some places.

These minerals seem in a great measure to replace the earthy cement. In descending a few feet further, the green fragments gradually decrease in number and become comparatively rare; the minerals also give place to the cement until the whole mass terminates below in a fine argillaceous substance, with an imperfect, slatey structure, and a Spanish-brown aspect.

This rock being much softer in its nature than the basalt, and more affected by decomposing agents, the number of fragments are, consequently, greater in proportion, and much more finely pulverized, forming the little soil which supports some of the scattered and scanty patches of the vegetation of these islands. The minerals embraced in this rock are generally confined to its upper part, where it unites and passes into the incumbent amygdaloid; many of them are also in common with that rock. They consist chiefly of quartz, crystalline and amorphous; amethyst, chalcedony, cachalong, agate, red jasper, felspar, zeolite, calcareous spar in rhombic crystals, sulphate of barytes, a minute crystal resembling black spinelle, sulphuret of iron, and green carbonate of copper.

The only appearance of an organized remain that I any where saw, was a fragment of carbonized wood, imbedded in this conglomerate. It was in a vertical position, about two and a half feet in length. and four inches in diameter; its colour is black, exhibiting a fine ligneous structure; the concentric circles are distinctly visible on its superior end; it occasionally gives sparks with steel, and effervesces slightly in nitric acid.

There are a number of active volcanoes in the vicinity of these islands, indications of which are daily seen in the pieces of pumice found strewed along the beach. Captain Weddel saw smoke issuing from the fissures of Bridgeman's Island, a few leagues to the N.E. of Palmer's Land, situated one degree south:—what little is known of it, which is only a small portion of its northern shore, contains several. Deception Island also, one of this group, has boiling springs, and a whitish substance like melted felspar, exudes from some of its fissures.

The rocky fragments on these islands are generally very hard, and little liable to the disintegrating influence of the atmosphere, and rarely, indeed, are they subject to a power capable of agitating them sufficiently to remove even the acuteness of their angles, consequently but a small quantity of soil can any where be found, and when discovered, being destitute of the necessary ingredients that give fatness to the earth elsewhere, it affords but a few scattered patches of vegetation, which appear to struggle hard for the small portion of vitality they enjoy. The Usnea fasciata, (Torry,) is most common. A species of polytrichum, resembling the alpinum of Linnæus, one or two lichens, and a fucus found in the sea, along the shores—when you add to these an occasional plant of a small species of avena, you complete the botanical catalogue of the islands.

The only vertebral animals ever observed on these islands are very few in number, and confined to the amphibia carnivora, of Cuvier; all being embraced in the genus Phoca. The P. leonina, Lin., (sea elephant,) is the largest of the species, sometimes attaining the length of twenty-five feet, and is regularly proportioned. These animals are remarkable for the powerful strength of their jaws. When attacked and wounded in such a manner as to be unable to reach the sea, in the struggle, either through agony or rage, they not unfrequently take up considerable sized stones with their mouth, and break them into a number of fragments between their teeth; and sometimes they seize upon the lance, breaking it instantaneously, or else bending it in such a manner as to render it perfectly useless. The sea leopard is not so large, but is a far more beautiful animal. P. vitulina, Lin. (fur seal.) This beautiful little animal was once most numerous here, but was almost exterminated by the sealers, at the time these islands were first discovered. There is also a fourth species, which I have no recollection of ever seeing the slightest notice of. It is probably not common, as I saw but one; it was standing on the extremities of its fore-feet, (flippers,) the head and chest perfectly erect, abdomen curved and resting on the ground; the tail was also in an upright position. The animal, in this attitude, bore a striking resemblance to the representations we frequently meet with of the "mermaid," and I think it was, undoubtedly, one of the animals of this genus that first gave origin to the fable of the maid of the sea. I regret that I could not obtain a nearer view of this interesting animal. When I approached within one hundred feet, it threw itself flat, and made rapidly for the sea. It appeared about twelve or fifteen feet in length, and distinctly more slender in proportion than any of the other species, so much so that the motion of the body, when moving, seemed perfectly undulating. Some of the seamen had seen them frequently on a former voyage, and mentioned

18*

that they were known among sealers by the name of sea-serpent from this circumstance. Some of the teeth were brought to me which had been picked up on the beach; the crown of the grinders is deeply and singularly five-lobed.

When these animals resort to the shores for the purpose of breeding, or shedding their hair, they are in fine condition. During this time they require no food, existing by the absorption of their fatty matter:—if killed at this period, you generally find a quantity of small stones in the stomach, swallowed most probably for the purpose of keeping that organ distended and preventing its internal surfaces from adhering to each other. When the season for returning to the sea arrives, these stones are ejected on the beach, and they proceed in search of their ordinary food, which is chiefly penguins.

A singular character in the habit of these animals is the faculty they possess of shedding tears when in any way molested.

The eyes become suffused, and the large tear-drops chasing each other in quick succession over their wrinkled faces, creates quite a sympathy in the breast of the beholder. Of the cetacea inhabiting the ocean, among these islands, the Balæna physalis, (fin whale,) with a smooth belly, is very numerous: the B. mysticeus, (right whale,) is occasionally seen. The grampus and dolphins are quite common, and a species of porpoise, which I had not before seen, occurs in great numbers. From their appearance in the water, their colour seemed dark, with a broad, somewhat waved, white line extending from the posterior and inferior part of the head, backward and upward to the dorsal fin; a second and similar one commences on the abdomen, immediately below the termination of the first, and ends at the origin of the tail, above. These marks are distinctly visible as they glide through the sea They are called sea-skunks by the sailors. I am told they are confined to high southern latitudes.

The birds which frequent these islands are much more numerous than any of the other classes of animals. Of penguins, there are five species. The Aptenodytes Patagonica, Lin. (king penguin,) is the largest and by far the most beautiful of the species, and may be seen in great numbers, covering the shores for some considerable extent. They are remarkably clean in their appearance; not a speck of any kind is suffered, for a moment, to sully the pure whiteness of the principal part of their plumage; their upright position, uniform cleanliness, and beautiful golden yellow cravat, contrasts finely with the dark back-ground by which they are relieved, so that the similitude is no inapt one, which compares them to a regiment of soldiers, immediately after parade. The females lay but one egg on the bare ground, which is rather larger than that of a goose, and of about equal value as an article of food, but differs a little in shape, being more tapering at its smaller end. The egg lies between the feet, the tail being sufficiently long to conceal it effectually from the sight. When approached, they move from you with a waddling gait, rolling it along over the smooth surface of the ground, so that a person, not acquainted with the fact, might pass through hundreds of them, without discovering it. The Spheniscus antarcticus, Shaw, (rookery penguin,) is more numerous than any of the other species, assembling together in vast congregations, occupying the smooth strips of plain for a mile or more in extent:—passing through them, they barely give you sufficient space, picking at your legs, and keeping up a continual chatter. Their whole appearance, as you walk along, brings powerfully to your recollection, the story of Gulliver, striding among the Lilliputians. The Cyhrsocoma saltator, C. torguata, C. catarractes, Shaw, are occasionally found along the beach, and scattered among the others. These birds swim with great velocity through the sea, and may be seen several feet in depth, shooting along in every direction; at short intervals rising to its surface, darting out again; at the same time uttering a quick sound, very similar to that produced by a single blast on a split quill Phalacrocorax graculus, Shaw, Sterna hirundo, (?) Lin. Diomedea exulans, Lin. and fuliginosa, Lath. Daption capense-antarcticum-niveum, Shaw, Fulmarius giganteus, and antarcticus, Shaw, are all very common. Procellaria pelagica, Lin.; this is much smaller than any I observed in other parts of the ocean, and may probably prove a distinct species: they build their nests in the crevices of the rocks, into which they generally deposit two eggs; and not unfrequently are they buried far beneath the drifting snows; however, they soon succeed in working for themselves a comfortable passage to the light of day. Larus eburneus? Gmel. Lestris catarractes, Tem. are also common. Chionis Forsteri, Shaw, (sheath bill.) This is the white pigeon, so often mentioned by mariners, as inhabiting the islands of the southern ocean; it is easily caught with the hand, and soon becomes domesticated. We kept a number of them several days, after leaving these islands; they ran about the decks of the vessel, apparently without any disposition to leave them, feeding from the hand of any individual that offered them food. The molusca are very few, though unique. An interesting species of pholas, a beautiful nucula, and a fine patella, neither of which I think have been described, comprise all that we saw.

The existence of a southern continent within the antarctic circle is, I conceive, a matter of much doubt and uncertainty; but, that there are extensive groups, or chains of islands, yet unknown, I think we have many indications to prove; and were I to express an opinion, I would say, that our course from the South Shetlands to the S. W., until we reached the 101° of west longitude, was at no great distance along the northern shores of one of these chains. The heavy clouds of mist which encircled us so often, could arise from no other cause than that of the influence of large quantities of snow or ice, on the temperature of the atmosphere; the hills of floating ice we encountered, could not form elsewhere than on the land. The drifting fuci we daily saw, grow only in the vicinity of rocky shores, and the penguins and terns that were almost at all times about us, from my observation of their habits, I am satisfied never leave the land at any great distance.

During our cruise to the south-west, above the 60° of south latitude, we found the current setting continually at a considerable rate towards the north-east, bearing the plants and ice along in its course, some of the latter embracing fragments of a rock, the existence of which we could discover no where on the islands we visited. When the westerly winds drew well towards the south, we were most generally enveloped in banks of fog, so dense that it was with difficulty we could distinguish objects at the distance of the vessel's length. When Palmer's Land becomes properly explored, together with the known islands, situated between the longitude of Cape Horn and that of Good Hope, I think they will prove to be the north-eastern termination of an extensive chain, passing near where Captain Cook's progress was arrested by the firm fields of ice, in latitude, 71° 10′ S., and west longitude, about 105°; had that skilful navigator succeeded in penetrating this mass of ice, he would unquestionably, in a short time, have made the land upon which it was formed. Captain Weddel, after passing the icy barrier to the east of the South Shetlands, succeeded in reaching the 74° 15′ south, (the highest latitude ever obtained by man,) and found, in crossing this chain, and progressing towards the south, that the sea became more free of ice, and the weather almost as mild as summer; evidently proving, I think, that the south pole can be nearly approached, without incurring any great degree of hazard in the attempt. But, for further information on the practicability of reaching the south pole, I must refer to the judicious remarks of Captain Edmund Fanning, of New-York, contained in his account of several voyages to the southern ocean, with which I perfectly coincide; and will conclude with regret, that the Government of the United States, with a population whose daring enterprise has already carried our flag into the remotest corners of the globe, could not yet (October, 1835,) be induced to forward an expedition, the expense of which would little exceed that of a vessel doubling Cape Horn.

They might thus settle this interesting question, and also determine, with certainty, the situation, magnitude, and extent of these lands, and by that means open a new source of revenue to the country, in the oil and fur of animals which must necessarily exist in these high southern regions.

PART VII.

AN ACCOUNT OF THE NOTED AND BLOODY NAVAL BATTLE FOUGHT ON THE 22D OF SEPTEMBER, 1779, BETWEEN THE GOOD MAN RICHARD, UNDER THE COMMAND OF JOHN PAUL JONES; AND THE SERAPIS, COMMANDED BY CAPTAIN PARSON.* BY AN OFFICER IN THE UNITED STATES' NAVY, TO WHOM CHANCE GAVE A STATION IN THE BATTLE, THAT CONSPICUOUSLY TENDED TO THE VICTORY. WITH THE GALLANT CAPTAIN PARSON'S HONOURABLE AND LIBERAL REMARKS TO CAPTAIN JONES ON THE RESULT.

The ships appear in sight of each other—Preparations for battle—The Serapis hails—Laconic answer of Jones—Battle commences—Lower deck guns burst — Serapis rakes the G. M. Richard — Dreadful and sweeping slaughter of G. M. Richard's marines—Ships run foul of each other—Serapis drops her anchor—G. M. Richard's Staff and Ensign knocked into the sea—Both ships attempt to board, in turn are driven back—Both ships on fire —Daring bravery of officer and men of main-top—Slaughtering effect of a hand grenade—Surrender of the Serapis—Humane, honourable, and liberal remarks of Captain Parsons—Dead bodies of the slain—Bloody carnage on the decks—The G. M. Richard abandoned—She sinks, head downwards—Whirlpool and narrow escape of boat—Arrival in the Texel—The sequel.

* It is believed, that such a particular and correct account of this

THE following detail of this noted naval battle is as given by this gallant officer. The author of this work has deemed its insertion would be interesting to the general reader, although of such ancient date.

The narrator was in the rank of midship man on board of the Good Man Richard, and called to the honour of acting, previous to the battle, as private secretary to Commodore Jones; but it was in this case thought requisite, in his mind, to place the narrator in the com mand of the main-top, with fifteen sharp shooters and four seamen, with the direction to pay no attention in their fire, or missiles, on the enemy's decks until they had cleared her tops of their men. Encouraged by the words of Captain Jones, he repaired with this force to the command of the main-top, to see what could be done for the honour of our country,

noted battle has never yet been presented to the public. It was found among this officer's papers after his decease.

Rate of metal, and' force of each ship.

GOOD MAN RICHARD, an old line-of-battle ship, (21 years of age,) cut down to a razee, and 402 men.—On her lower-gun-deck, six eighteen-pounders. On gun-deck, twenty-eight twelve and nine-pounders. On quarter-deck and spar-deck, six six-pounders.

SERAPIS, a new ship, recently off the stocks, and 308 men.—On lower gun-deck, twenty eighteen-pounders. On upper gun-deck, twenty nine-pounders. On quarter-deck and forecastle, ten six-pounders.

and the national flag of stars and stripes flying over them.

The action commenced seven minutes past eight, P. M., and lasted four hours and eight minutes.

At four, P. M., on the 22d of September, 1779, the two ships came in sight of each other, the Good Man Richard having in com pany the Alliance and Pallais frigates. The only consort of the Serapis was the Countess of Scarborough, a ship of only twenty-two guns, which, after a few broadsides, surrendered to the Pallais frigate. After sighting the enemy's ships, signal was immediately displayed from the commodore's ship, the Good Man Richard, to the squadron, for a general chase, when in a few minutes before 8, P.M., we had nearly closed within hailing distance of the enemy, which now plainly showed her double row of teeth. Orders were now given by the commodore to haul up our courses, and clew up the top-gallant sails; at same time directing, by signal, for the Alliance to support us. At first she kept aloof out of gun-shot, and afterwards, when she came up, she so badly performed as to do us more hurt than she did the enemy. The Pallais was also directed to attack the small ship. The enemy now hailed thus:—"What ship is that?" The answer from Captain Jones was:—"Come a little nearer and I'll tell you!" The enemy instantly commenced the fight by a broadside from her upper tier, we returning it with ours, as well as musquetry, &c. In a few minutes we were convinced that the ship we had engaged was a two-decker, and more than our match, as we had by this time received several of her eighteen pound shot, through and through our ship; and to add to our hard fortune, the first time three of our eighteens were discharged, they burst, killing the most of the men that were stationed at them. In consequence of this, Captain Jones sent orders to the lieutenant of this division not to discharge another of the eighteen-pounders, but to promptly abandon them.

The wind being now very light, and the enemy finding that she could out sail us, made use of this advantage and ran under our stern, raked us fore and aft, killed the main part of the marines that were stationed on the poop, and obliged the colonel that commanded them, with the surviving ones, to abandon it, besides doing much damage in the other parts of the ship. From this she ran athwart our fore-foot, (after discharging her broadside, and giving us an opportunity of returning the same,) raked us a second time, and killed a number of our men; in fine, she galled us in this manner so confoundedly, that orders were given to lay her aboard; accordingly, as she passed our fore-foot, we ran our jib-boom between her mizen shrouds and starboard mizen whang:—Captain Jones at the same time in an audible voice, said, "That's well, my lads!—we've got her now!" The enemy, finding that they were foul of us, endeavoured to get clear, by letting go an anchor, but the wind dying away she swung round upon us, and carried away our ensign-staff and ensign, both falling into the sea, with her jib-boom; her jib-stay being now cut away aloft, fell in upon our poop, which Captain Jones, and the sailing master made fast to our mizen-mast. The firing had not ceased during these manœuvres except the cannon *a-mid-ships*, which now could not be worked or managed *on board either ship*. Several attempts were now made to board the enemy, but they did not succeed. The enemy also endeavoured to board us, and actually came on board, but were beaten back, and our men pursued them on board their ship, and were again repulsed in their turn; for we both lay so near together that it was an easy matter to step from one ship on board the other.

It now fell entirely calm, and the enemy having an anchor down, we both rode to it with the current, we being then about a league from Flamborough Head. The action had now been commenced about three hours and a quarter, when the enemy's tops were silenced, and we now directed our fire upon their decks with much success; about this time the enemy's light sails got on fire, this communicated to her rigging, and from thence to ours. Thus, were both ships on fire at one and the same time. Therefore, the firing on both sides ceased till it was extinguished by the contending parties. The action then began anew, and was continued sharply on both sides, when our carpenter went and told the gunner that our ship had four feet of water in her hold, that Captain Jones was killed, and all the rest of the officers that ranked above him, and that the only way for them to save their lives would be to go upon deck—call for quarters, and haul down our colours. Upon this the gunner and carpenter made haste to get on deck, and were joined on their way thither by the master-at-arms. As soon as they had got upon the quarter deck, they cried, "Quarters! quarters! for God's sake quarters!—our ship is sinking." From this they mounted the poop with a design of hauling down the ensign, but finding them missing they descended to the pendant halyards, where they were met by Captain Jones, he being upon the forecastle when they first came upon deck; hearing these fellows halloo for quarters, he cried out thus:—"What cowardly rascals are these? shoot 'em, kill 'em!" Having met with them, his pistols having been previously discharged, he sent them with all his force at these poltroons, who immediately knew Jones, and fled below. Two of them were badly wounded in the head with Jones' pistols. Both ships now took fire again, and on board of ours it had communicated to the main top, so that we were in the greatest consternation imaginable for some time, and it was not without some difficulty we quenched it.

The enemy now cried, "If you ask quarters, why don't you strike your pendant?"—"Aye, aye," said our commodore, "we'll do it when we can fight no longer, but expect to see you strike first." Having now began the action afresh, it was continued with redoubled vigour on both sides. The two ships now lay alongside each other with their yards locked, and having cleared the enemy's tops of their men, this gallant officer, in daring bravery, now led his men under his command, across on the ship's yards, and into the Serapis' top, and then directing their fire, with hand grenades, and other missiles, down on her decks, causing so much slaughter, as that in half an hour they could net perceive a single man of the enemy above deck. They, however, kept playing four of their starboard bow guns into us, which still annoyed us, and which induced us in our main-top gang, to redouble our activity in the further able and effective acts which succeeded in driving their men from their stations at those before-mentioned guns, on their gun deck, in spite of their officers, and which acts were admitted as prominent in obtaining the victory. Thus, at length one of our hand grenades being thrown by us, from the top, fell upon the enemy's upper gun-deck—from this, it rebounded, and fell between decks, where it set fire to some powder which lay scattered upon the enemy's lower gun-deck, and blew up (as we subsequently learned), about seventeen of them. This threw them into confusion, and as they were upon the point of crying for quarters—the Alliance unexpectedly made her appearance, and began a heavy fire upon us, as well as on the enemy, which at first, made some of our officers, as well as men, imagine that she was an English ship of war.

The signals of reconnoissance was now ordered to be made on board of our ship, which was three lanthorns placed in a horizontal line upon the fore, main, and mizen shrouds, to undeceive the Alliance ; as she had by this time killed eleven of our men, and wounded several others, by raking us; notwithstanding, we did at the first hail her, and told them that she was firing on the wrong ship. A few minutes after this accident, (although most of the officers of the Good Man Richard, and some belonging to the Alliance, think it was done *designedly*,*) and about a quarter past twelve, we were pleased with the crying out of "Quarters! quarters!" by our enemy. We immediately boarded the enemy's ship. Thus ended this long and bloody fight, we having lost on our part one hundred and sixty men killed, mortally wounded, and missing. On the part of the enemy, one hundred and thirty-eight men were killed, and died of their wounds—which were the number of lives lost in both ships. And those exclusive also of the wounded that recovered. Our prize proved to be the Serapis, commanded by Captain Parson, who, after he had surrendered to us, with his lieutenant and other officers, came on board of our ship and inquired for Captain Jones, for it seems he had been informed who commanded our ship. When they met, Captain Parson accosted his anta-

* Landais, the captain of the Alliance, (a Frenchman,) and Captain Jones, were bitter enemies to each other, and it is thought that Landais took this opportunity of revenging himself on his mortal enemy.

gonist thus, presenting him his sword, " 'T is not without the greatest reluctance that I resign to you this, for of all men upon the face of the globe, 't is you that I hate the worst." Jones took his sword, saying, "You have fought like a hero, and I make no doubt your sovereign will reward you in a most ample manner for it." Captain Parson then asked our commodore of what his crew consisted, mostly Frenchmen, or Americans? "Americans," said the latter, "well," said the former, "then it has been diamond cut diamond with us—a desperate family fight,—brother against brother, for," said he, "I must own, that I think the Americans equally as brave as the English."

The Serapis had lost her main and mizen masts during the engagement, the former having been cut almost entirely off, by our shot, on a level with her gang-way, and having fallen overboard, as we swung from alongside of her.

We were now alarmed in having two enemies to encounter, almost as formidable as the one we had just conquered, viz. fire and water, we could not keep our ship free with all the pumps, and as many hands as could go to and work at them, but she kept gaining upon us, every minute, which was no great cause of surprise, we having received several shot between wind and water, (and some of these breaches could not be come at.) The fire had also communicated itself to several parts of the ship, where it being dry and rotten, it was found impracticable to extinguish it. In the dilemma, our commodore ordered the signal of distress to be made, and the Alliance, Pallais, and Vengeance brig, sent their boats to our assistance, when the commodore embarked, with Captain Parson, in one of them, and went on board of the Serapis, leaving orders with the narrator and another midshipman, to get all the powder up out of the magazine, and see that it was sent on board of the other ships of the squadron, together with all the wounded men, prisoners, &c.; and after having executed these orders, to abandon the Good Man Richard. The fire had now communicated itself to several parts, and burned with amazing rapidity within one foot of the magazine. Having got the powder and wounded men sent off, the prisoners (to the number of about fifty) made an attempt to take the ship from us, there being then on board but about twenty of our crew. They had made themselves master of our quarter-deck and forecastle, braced round the yards, and got her before the wind, with a design to run her ashore. In consequence of this another battle ensued; but having the greater part of the arms in our possession, (suitable for a close fight,) we soon got to be masters of the ship again, after killing two of them, and wounding several others.

When the boats came alongside again, we caused these desperate fellows to be, by them, conducted on board of the Pallais. After the action had ceased, it was not thought advisable to despatch either of the squadron after the fleet of merchantmen in sight, whose convoy we had captured, as the situation of the Good Man Richard *then* needed the assistance of the *whole* of our squadron. Having now executed the orders of the commodore, left with us, we thought of leaving the poor Good Man Richard to the mercy of the waves.

However, before doing so, I went down into the gun room with some men, to see to the embarkation of the officers' trunks which had been deposited here; but, alas, what havoc! not a piece of one of them could be found as large as a continental dollar bill; it is true, several shirts, coats, &c., were found, but so shockingly were they pierced, and cut in pieces with the enemy's shot, that they were not worth carrying off. There was such a breach from one side of the gun room to the other, that, (in the common way of speaking,) a coach and six could have passed through it

The number and bulk of splinters were prodigious, many of them as fine as carpenters' chips. After this, and taking a survey of the dead bodies that were scattered about the decks, I could not help shuddering at the horrid sight. The blood which had issued from them covered the decks in such a manner, that it was over shoe in several places. This dreadful sight, I must confess, sickened the heart with feelings against ever battling again with our fellow-men, to such bloody destruction of human life. Upon the whole, I think, this slaughtering fight, may with propriety be said to have been a scene of carnage on *both sides.*

During the action, the enemy had thrown into our gun-room a number of loose cannon cartridges, in order, as they afterwards owned, to blow us up. With the destruction of the officers' trunks, the narrator lost all his wearing apparel; and those remaining on his back, at the close of the battle, were partly burned, in the act of extinguishing the several fires, especially those of the tops and rigging.

We thought of nothing now but of abandoning the Good Man Richard, that was soon to serve so many as a sea coffin, and embarked accordingly in the boats, and soon after arrived alongside of the Serapis. Here Captain Jones ordered me not to get out of the boat, but to receive two or three additional men, and to promptly return back on board of the Poor Man Richard, for, said he, in such a part of my cabin you'll find such, and such papers—go and bring them, and make no tarry. These orders I went to carry into effect if possible; the Good Man Richard was then lying head to the wind with her topsails aback. I shot up with my boat under her stern, and was just a-going to lay her alongside, when I perceived the water run in and out of her lower ports. This somewhat staggered and brought me to a stand, but very soon, finding our situation dangerous, I ordered the men to use their oars in backing off from her. We thus had got, I judged, about three rods from her, when she fetched a heavy pitch and disappeared instantaneously; but although we were now under brisk sternway, gaining fast some farther rods from her, yet the agitation of the sea and its waves, with the whirlpool, was such that we came near sharing the same fate, and going down with her.

Thus, sinking head downwards, went to the bottom the Good Man Richard, about four hours after her crew had taken possession of her prize; and it was a thankful relief to us, to safely step on the Serapis' deck on our return to her.

We now went to work, and in a very short time we had got jury masts erected, and sail enough spread to shape our course for the Texel, in Holland, the wind being *contrary* to steer for France. On the 3d of October we arrived with our little squadron, and prizes, at the Texel. Just as we came to anchor, we discovered in the offing an English sixty-four gun ship and three frigates; these had, as we subsequently learned, been despatched in pursuit of us, as soon as the English had got intelligence of our squadron being upon their coast.

In a proper time after the action, Commodore Jones, in presence of his officers, mentioned, as highly praise-worthy, those daring and brave acts of the command of the Good Man Richard's main top; and subsequently handed to this brave officer the following certificate to the American Congress:—

CERTIFICATE TO CONGRESS.*

I do hereby certify, that Nathaniel Fanning, of Stonington, State of Connecticut, has sailed with me in the station of midshipman eighteen months, while I commanded the Good Man Richard, until she was lost in the action with the Serapis, and in the Alliance, and Ariel frigates. His bravery on

* This evidence of American bravery was forwarded by the author to His Excellency President Van Buren, and no doubt will rest on the files in the Department at Washington.

board the first-mentioned ship, in the action with the Serapis, a King's ship of fifty guns, off Flamborough Head, while he had command of the main top, will, I hope, recommend him to the notice of Congress in the line of promotion, with his other merits.

JOHN PAUL JONES.

L'Orient, (in France,) December 17th, 1780.

NOTE.—This brave and gallant officer, Lieutenant Nathaniel Fanning, of the United States' Navy, (a brother of the author of Fanning's Voyages,) mentioned in this certificate, and bloody battle of unusual carnage, like the ever-to-be-lamented and notedly-brave Commodore O. H. Perry, of U. S. Navy, was brought to the grave by an attack of the yellow-fever, while on active duty in command at the United States' naval station at Charleston, S. C., on the 30th day of September 1805.

PART VIII.

NARRATIVE SKETCH OF AN OCCURRENCE THE MOST BARBAROUS, FROM THE VOYAGE OF THE AMERICAN BRIGANTINE HERSILIA OF STONINGTON, CAPTAIN JAMES P. SHEFFIELD, TO THE SOUTH SEAS, UNDER THE DIRECTIVE AGENCY OF THE AUTHOR, IN THE YEAR 1821.

CHAPTER I.

Hersilia sails from New South Shetlands—Anchors at Isle St. Mary's—Her capture—Barbarian chief Beneviades—His cruel treatment of crew while prisoners—Town and river Arauco on coast of Chili—Prisoners' sufferings and hard fare in rations—Military duty—The tyrant chief and American sentry—Parade of the royal army—General Beneviades' eulogy on the Americans, and reprimand to his officers—Paper money—Death to refuse its tender—Disgusting and barbarous punishment of females—Inhuman execution of a Padre.

THE following narration is, as given the author, by Captain Sheffield, and corroborated in the main by that very worthy mariner, Captain David Kellogg, junior, who also refers (to his colleague in their sufferings) to that able and gentlemanly commander, Captain W. E. Hoxie, now in the command of the line packet ship, the North America :—

THE Hersilia having obtained a cargo of fur seal skins at the South Shetland Isles, and having a favourable opportunity, shipped them home; and then, agreeably to the instructions given by the agent to her commander, she sailed on the 24th of February, 1821, from these Islands for the Pacific, with the view and intention of procuring another cargo, and thereby making a double voyage during the same trip. Further, by their successful seal hunting they obtained and completed their second cargo of 15,000 seal skins, and were then in May, 1821, at anchor in the Hersilia, in the North Bay at the Island of St. Mary's, situated on the coast of Chili. Having now finished their hunting excursions, and the taking of seals, they were preparing for sea, to depart on their passage home; when, nearly ready, on the point of weighing anchor, and expecting certainly in a few hours to sail on their passage to double Cape Horn, on their return with their second valuable cargo, they were suddenly surprised, and their vessel, their heretofore so fortunate and charming little Hersilia taken, and themselves made prisoners, by a gang of ruffians calling themselves soldiers, belonging to the army, and under the orders of that barbarian chief, General Beneviades, who was at this time in command of the royal Spanish army, then encamped opposite to St. Mary's Isle, on the main land of Chili. His head quarters were at Arauco, a walled town, situa ted a short distance up in the country from the mouth of the river of the same name. The mouth of this river having at it a sand bar, afforded no harbour for vessels of burden, as only their pereaugos could pass over, and into the river, owing to the shallow water on the bar; vessels of burthen having business with the town, or up the river, were obliged to anchor in the road off, and without the bar. The Hersilia's two boats were on shore at Isle St. Mary's when captured with her officers, and all her crew, (excepting five that remained with the captain on board,) where they had had on shore a washing day in the preparation of their duds, for a sea passage home, when, as they were on the point of embarking themselves and effects in their boats, to repair on board of their brig, they were on a sudden surprised by this gang from their ambush, of thirty-six pirate soldiers, a detachment from the Grand Royal Army, under the command of the before mentioned chief Beneviades, in charge, and conducted by a stony-hearted, inhuman officer, by name Crayro. They had come over from the Main, and landed on another part of the island, and thus, at 8 P. M. on the 14th of May, 1821, in the dusk of the evening, they surprised the Hersilia's men with a charge upon them by loaded musquets, and at the point of the bayonet forced them up on the beach from their boats, where they were very roughly treated; and after being thus made prisoners, and all bound hand and foot, they were threatened by the guard set over them with instant death if they made any noise, lest it should alarm Captain Sheffield and those on board the brig. Matters on shore being thus accomplished and arranged by these freebooters, their pirate leader, Crayro, embarking twelve of his men in each of our boats, proceeded off to capture and get possession of the Hersilia. The boats, one on each side of her, boarded her at one and the same time. Thus, in turn, was the unsuspecting captain and those on board with him, surprised by the unwelcome "Halloo!" in ruffian tones, "you are our prisoners!" They ordered Captain Sheffield to be silent, and with the charged musquet at his breast, and suspended sword over his head, to repair instantly as a prisoner to his state-room, where a sentry was set over him, and at the same time the men were driven at the point of the bayonet down into the forecastle. What a change of feelings these innocent American mariners must now have felt, from those of an hour previous! Having completed their valuable cargo, and just on the point of sailing for home, to thus meet with such a severe rebuff! What a weight of the most agonizing feeling must at the time have preyed on the mind of their worthy commander, while reflecting, a prisoner in his state-room! The reader can well judge, as all, all their flattering and pleasing hopes were thus blasted, and so suddenly changed into the severe and heart-aching contrary.

These barbarians having thus made the capture of the vessel, and all on board, or belonging to her, proceeded with the boats to bring the bound prisoners off from the shore on board, when they tumbled them in such a rough, unfeeling manner down below deck, as if they were sacks of carpenters' chips.

They then got the brig under way and steered her over across the bay for the mouth of the river Arauco, where they anchored her in the road, just without the bar, making across the mouth of the river, when they very promptly took Captain Sheffield, with all the officers and crew, (except Mr. Daniel W. Clark, our first officer, whom they retained on board to navigate her for them in such employment as their tyrant general should thereafter please direct,) forthwith on shore. Having now unbound them, they marched them directly off as prisoners under a strong guard of a fresh detachment for their head quarters, at the town of Arauco. On their arrival at that station, they were very quickly paraded into the presence of their general, Beneviades; also being present their second in command, by name Picco, a more hard-hearted, brutal, unfeeling savage, if possible, than his senior, Beneviades, and several other officers of this royal army, so by them called.

Beneviades, now setting Captain Sheffield and a young seaman, Rogers by name, apart from the others to wait on his dictatorial person, he then caused all the others to be distributed one to each officer, to wait on, and serve them at their quarters, or in their families, as a menial slave; charging them at the time to remain content, on their peril, and likewise on such allowance of rations as this stone-hearted, *humane* general should thereafter please to direct. This subsequently proved, in not averaging daily, during the whole time they remained in this servile imprisonment, over half a pound of meat to each person, and that beef, as they called it, but it mostly came from the carcase of the jack, or mule, with a despicable, mean, limited proportion of vegetables; these they were, it is true, by unfeeling tyrants, permitted to cook, as they could, or eat them raw, if they could not in their confined limits procure their own fuel; an article was also given in small black rolls of the coarsest kind, supposed to be made from a mixture of barley and beans, said by them to be bread; they, however, obtained some of this only once or twice a week. This, those truly suffering Americans assert, was their regular fare in provisions for their subsistence, but a full allowance of fresh water was granted to them, on their going to the spring for it. To add to this hard fare, the worst of usage and daily curses were heaped on them. In sustaining life, by such scanty and miserable daily rations, they not only had to labour hard during the day, like menial servants for their masters, but were also forced to do military duty, in their turns, on sentry through the night. The author here takes pride in mentioning an evidence showing how well and patriotically those suffering citizens from Stonington supported the American national character during their unjust and severe imprisonment.

Kellogg and his shipmate, by name Stanton, being in middle time of night, on sentry, at each of their different posts, when Beneviades, in disguise, as was his frequent practice of going the rounds at different times during the night, to satisfy his mind as to the watchful alertness of the sentries, came up within a rod's distance of Kellogg, requesting of him in a familiar manner to be permitted to pass, Kellogg, in answer, told him to advance and give the counter-sign, Beneviades hesitated, then said, he was their general, Kellogg promptly and sternly answered, "I am aware of my duty, I know you not now as such," at the same time charging with the point of his lance within a foot of Beneviades' breast, he more firmly said, "give me the counter-sign before you stir a step, or you are a dead man," Beneviades instantly gave him the counter-sign, threw off his disguise so far as to make himself truly known to Kellogg, observing to him, that he was a true and good soldier, and then passed on. On his coming to the place where Stanton was posted, he met with the like reception; but, on the contrary with his own soldiers, mostly all let him pass without giving the counter-sign, on his observing to them, as he had to Kellogg, that he was their general, two excepted, whom he found asleep.

On the next day, when his army was on parade, he ordered his officers, and Captain Sheffield and his crew to the centre, informed them of his tour on the rounds in the night, told of his reception by the different sentries, spoke in the highest praise of his confidence and the dependence he could place in Captain Sheffield and his Americans ; then severely reprimanded his officers for their neglect of discipline, and charge to their veteran soldiers, as he called them; as for instance, a serious fault had been committed during the past night, which he had just mentioned, when they were set on sentry. Then ordering the two unfortunates he found asleep on their posts, to be punished according to their offence, he dismissed the parade.

About this time Beneviades observing Captain Sheffield to be an expert and smooth penman, set him and Captain Morrison, of a Boston brig, which had been captured at Isle St. Mary's, in much the same manner as the Hersilia, but, subsequently, in July, about two months after the capture of the Hersilia, to making for him paper money, treasury bills, as this noted general and dictator called them. The bills were made from the sheet of white Spanish paper, which was cut into strips of about the size of ordinary bank bills, and then by Captain Sheffield, encircled by flourishes with the pen. Within these flourishes were written the amount, and date, and the bills were made payable to the bearer, at his treasury, *when in funds*, to be paid out of the military chest of the army. Thus prepared, they

21

were signed by Beneviades, as commander-in-chief for *Del' Rey*, (the king,) and countersigned by Captain Sheffield, as financial secretary. A proclamation was then issued by Beneviades from head-quarters, making this paper of treasury bills a lawful tender, and the punishment of a refusal of it, corporeal or death, as this barbarian tyrant chief should be pleased to sentence, whenever reported by any complaint to him.

Our narrators saw two decent and worthy married women, in a state of nudity, publicly whipped through the streets, and also a priest as publicly shot, by the decree, sentence, and order of this bloody, unfeeling monster, for refusing this paper money.

CHAPTER II.

Hersilia fitted out a cruiser—Her return from cruise off Chiloe Island—Violent storm—Hersilia wrecked in storm—Her captain and crew employed to launch her afloat again—Whale boats—Daring and desperate enterprise of Captain Sheffield and crew—Plan of escape—Brave acts of Kellogg and Hoxie—The prisoners escape—Land on Island St. Mary's—Forced to subsist on raw seals' flesh.

On Captain Sheffield and crew being removed from their vessel, she was immediately discharged, and her cargo put into some store huts on the ridge of the beach near to the chops of the mouth of the river, some heavy cannon were mounted on her deck, and she was fitted out as a royal cruiser of war, manned with about one hundred officers and men, mostly taken from their army ranks, all under the command of a colonel. Mr. Clark was forced to navigate her wherever this colonel and commanding officer should direct, under penalty of death if he hesitated or refused.

She sailed to cruise off and along the coast, and to put into St. Carlos, in the Island of Chiloe, for provisions and specie, to be received from the governor of that colony for the army of Beneviades. She was several weeks engaged on this cruise and service, and then returned to Arauco with her cargo of specie, &c. However, in a few days after again anchoring in Arauco Road, there began to blow a norther, which soon increased to a heavy gale, and drove our beautiful, captured Hersilia, from her anchors and on shore, where she remained at low water, high and dry, on the beach. After this gale had subsided, and we had again fair weather, Beneviades consulted with Captain Sheffield on the prospect of getting the brig off the beach again ; and on proceeding to a survey of her situation with this famous general, Captain

Sheffield observed eight whale boats, on the river's banks near its mouth, and not far from the place where the brig lay. Messrs. Fuller and Horn, with three seamen, had, while they were set at work, at a previous time, by the river's mouth, escaped in such a craft, and got clear of their slavery; although at the time, this occurrence made our tyrant general raving mad, threatening to immediately execute the captain and all his remaining crew then with his army, should he discover thereafter, that they had any knowledge at the time of their comrades going, or intention to thus escape. In fact, the corroborating narrators heard this bloody-minded, and savage chief, Beneviades, frequently threaten Captain Sheffield with the execution of him, and his men, if they did not prove true to him, and also attentive to their duty, and industrious to his wish; this threat was to be expected sure, to be put promptly into execution if they failed in their escape. Notwithstanding all this, the discovery of these boats favoured his and the men's wishes for a chance to put into operation their plan for endeavouring to escape from this suffering, iron tyranny. Therefore, in the best judged policy, Captain Sheffield observed to Beneviades, that his soldiers did not understand, nor could the work be done by, or with them, but, if he was disposed to furnish him with a number of the empty tight casks from the whale ships he had previously captured, (an English whale ship, and the Hero, a whale ship of Nantucket,) and with all his crew of seamen and artificers, he believed he could get her afloat again, after a few days' work. To this Beneviades consented, (except the Hersilia's carpenter and armourer, Messrs. Guard and Gallop,) these two, he said, were so much needed there by the army, that he would not consent to let them go from the army encampment, on any occasion. Captain Sheffield thinking it not good policy to insist on them, did not press it. Accordingly, on the next morning, their crew (except the two retained) were mustered with their captain, and marched down under an officer and guard to the poor, cast-away Hersilia, and by their good captain, set cheerfully at work shovelling the sand away and placing under her bottom the empty casks. They did not hurry in this work, but rather prolonged it, in the wish to gain time to effect a plan of escape, by putting into execution the following daring and very desperate enterprise. Those entrusted with the secret were Captain Sheffield, the first officer, Mr. D. W. Clark, a Mr. Lane, mate of the Boston brig, captured by Beneviades, and eight others of the Hersilia's crew; these were the number entrusted with their important secret and intention to gain life and liberty, or submit to death. They were urged on to this course principally by hard usage and fare, and all were solemnly pledged to each other to effect their escape, or sacrifice their lives in the trial. Among these determined Americans, stood conspicuous Hoxie and Kellogg, who were appointed on the particular look-out, and to notify and report when a favourable opportunity should occur to move on their plan, with the view of escape from their slavery. The soldiers of their guard were quartered in a long shed of a building erected upon the beach near the bank of the river's mouth, adjacent to which lay hauled up five of the eight whale boats, three others were across the river hauled up on the opposite bank of it, the two officers that had charge of, and commanded the guard, being quartered in a small hut nearly joining to the soldier's quarters. The previous and recent conduct and behaviour of the Americans, had established confidence, and put greatly at rest all suspicion of any intention to escape, so much so, as to induce the commanding officer to suspend setting his sentries at their different posts on guard during the night, and to let the soldiers now sleep all in their quarters. The two officers only in turn keeping watch, sitting at the door of their hut, and only calling out a patrole guard of the soldiers every four hours, merely to march the rounds, and then direct back into their quarters to sleep. Thus, affairs were proceeding on, when, shortly after midnight, on the 26th of September, 1821, Hoxie and Kellogg reported to Captain Sheffield, that a favourable opportunity had arrived, and all their guard were believed to be now asleep: their party mustered without noise, but, on a second reconnoitre, the officer was discovered to be awake, which caused them to remain still, but, in great anxiety lest the present opportunity should pass away, by the breaking of the day; accordingly, between 3 and 4 A. M., it was proposed to take prisoner the officer awake, so as not to give any alarm that should awake his comrade or the guard. Kellogg, with true American spirit, volunteered for this act, and armed with an uplifted axe, stole softly up to him, and in a low voice of firm sternness, but such as not to awake or rouse the other officer, or guard, informed him that he was his prisoner, and that if he attempted to stir, or speak, he would instantly hew the life out of him; he remained thus with upheld axe over him, until Captain Sheffield and the others had selected two boats, launched them, procured the oars, and staved all the other boats on the bank of the river, and Mr. Clark, with his boat, had crossed and landed Hoxie on the opposite bank, who boldly and quickly staved all the boats hauled up on that bank, this was done to prevent an immediate pursuit of them; all being now in the two boats ready for the start, with their oars manned ready for the stroke, Captain Sheffield, with the bow of his boat just touched to the shore, gave the daring Kellogg the signal to come and embark, who, cautioning his prisoner, at his peril, to keep still, bid him a good morning, and alertly stepped forward and into the boat awaiting him, when both boats instantly sprung on their oars, swiftly passing down for the mouth of the river; however, before the boats had got out of sight of the guards' quarters, the officer had awaked and mustered out his soldiers, but by this time the boats had got at so long a gun-shot on their way, that they did not think proper to fire after them. On arriving at the mouth of the river, they crossed the bar with some risk, owing to the then unfavourable time of tide, and surf on it, but their good fortune favouring them, they passed safely over, when they shaped their course across the bay for the Isle of St. Mary's, but before they were able to reach over to the island's shore, a northern gale blew up, which soon increased into a violent storm, that continued and detained them on the island until the sixth day. This time was very severely trying to their minds, for although it prevented Beneviades sending at present any detachment after them, still it gave to him time to repair the stoven boats, and thereby enable him to send in pursuit after them as soon as the storm should sufficiently abate. They were, therefore, very anxious to proceed to a place where they would be surely clear, and out of fear of him and his unfeeling warriors. Also, they could here procure nothing to subsist upon but raw seals' flesh, and wild fruits.

CHAPTER III.

Boats put out to sea—Their suffering in them during their voyage—Effect a landing at Moula on the coast of Chili —Kind treatment and reception from the inhabitants—Travel to Valparaiso—United States' consul—U. S. frigate Constellation, kindness of her gallant commander and officers—British flag ship, 74—And sloop of war—Generous and noble proceedings of the British Admiral, Sir T. M. Hardy.

However, on the sixth day, the storm having abated, and having provided a quantity of seals' flesh for sea stores, they launched forth and left the island, steering out to sea in their small and tender craft, holding a course to the northward for Valparaiso, but, having a care in not coming near to the Chilian coast until they had well past Talcahuanna, and the Bay of Conception, lest some of Beneviades' armed craft should be there watching off that port for them; being thus at sea in those small boats until the third day, without water, and their meat becoming quite putrid and offensive, with the bad weather and rough sea, caused by the late storm, which kept them almost constantly wet, thus, their sufferings were indeed severe, but were supported in bearing them by the consolation that they had thus escaped. During the squalls of wind and rain in the second night the two boats were separated, and on the next day the one in which was the first officer and party, put in for the coast and shore of Chili, and succeeded in effecting a landing near to the small town of Moula, situated on this coast. The other, in which was the captain and party, succeeded in effecting a landing some miles farther northward on the same coast, but some leagues to the south of Valparaiso. Both parties then travelled by land to that city. They were at both places on landing received with much kindness and well treated by the Chilian inhabitants, as also at the towns and villages on their travel through the country to Valparaiso, the inhabitants freely contributing to their wants and comfort in provisions (which now tasted to them like a Connecticut thanksgiving treat,) and necessaries; and to all appearance manifesting much good feeling towards them in their late sufferings.

On their arrival at Valparaiso they were received with true fatherly kindness and attention by the United States' Consul, Michael Hogan, Esquire. There were at moorings in the harbour the United States' frigate Constellation, the gallant commander and officers of which were very kind to them; and also a British 74, and sloop of war, under Commodore Sir T. M. Hardy, the senior officer now in command of Her Britannic Majesty's squadron on the Pacific station. As soon as Admiral Hardy was informed of the arrival of Captain Sheffield, his officers and men, and of their sufferings, and escape from that barbarian chief, Beneviades, as also their distressful situation, he promptly, with the noblest and most humane feelings, sent an officer on shore with an invitation to Captain Sheffield, saying, that he should be much pleased to receive him on board his ship. With this invitation Captain Sheffield immediately complied, when he was by this venerable and worthy commodore most cordially received into his stately cabin, and gave the detail of his capture, and the sufferings they had experienced from Beneviades. After a few minutes consideration, the commodore asked if his vessel and crew belonged to Stonington, being answered in the affirmative, this gallant commodore then put the following questions to him: "Would there be, do you think, any probability, if you were assisted by a vessel of war, Captain Sheffield, of recovering the liberty of the remainder of your men, and your property from Beneviades?" "With such a force as you speak of, sir, under the orders of Commodore Hardy, I think Beneviades would deliver up the men to me, with the Hersilia's cargo; at any rate, thus situated and supported, I should be freely willing to put at risk, and in requisition, my person, time, and service, to try the experiment, should Commodore Hardy think the trial worth attempting." Then, without further loss of time in deliberation, this highly worthy commander sent an officer for the captain of the sloop of war, Conway, with orders to repair on board the flag-ship. On the captain's entering the cabin, the commodore said, "I have the pleasure to introduce to you, sir, Captain Sheffield, late in command of the American brig, Hersilia, who has been very unfortunate;" and then observed to him, thus, "You will, sir, receive Captain Sheffield on board of your ship as a passenger, and a friend of mine, with also such of his officers and men as he may choose to designate, and then proceed in your ship with all despatch, up the coast for Arauco, where you will anchor your ship in the road, and then use your best endeavours, consistent with His Majesty's service, in the aid to Captain Sheffield to obtain the liberation of the remainder of his men, and also his property, from the royal chief, Beneviades, receiving the same on board your vessel, and report all here to me, when accomplished, or when the trial in accordance with this order is made. Further, you will, sir, consider yourself responsible for the return of Captain Sheffield safe back here to me, without the slightest injury." Thus, handsomely and nobly, to the honour of the British navy, did this eminent British commander proceed, and act in this case, for the relief of those unfortunate and distressed mariners.

CHAPTER IV.

Captain Sheffield sails for Arauco in the British sloop of war, Conway—Anchor at Arauco—Town and store buildings in flames—A bloody battle—Patriot and royal armies—The defeated armies—Courteous and kind conduct of the commander of His B. M. sloop of war, Conway—Captain Sheffield and men return in the Conway to Valparaiso—Close of the narrative.

CAPTAIN Sheffield took leave of the gallant commodore, and repaired with her able commander on board the British sloop of war, Conway, which was soon under way on her trip up the coast of Chili for Arauco. After a very agreeable passage, on the fifth day thereafter, they brought the sloop at anchor in the road of Arauco. But, to their surprise, the town and store buildings at the mouth of the river, and even the beautiful little wrecked Hersilia on the beach, as well as the other vessels captured by the orders and force of this noted chief, Beneviades, were seen in flames, all, all rapidly consuming by the fire. On landing, they found the patriots in command, and were informed that a desperate and bloody battle had just been fought and decided between the patriot and royal armies, in which the latter, under Beneviades, had been defeated with much slaughter. He had then set fire to the town and store buildings which we saw in flames, and had retreated with his surviving force into the wilderness at the foot of the mountains. The store buildings wherein the cargo of the Hersilia, when captured, was deposited, were now burned, and the vessel likewise destroyed. Thus was lost to all concerned, this fine new American brig Hersilia, together with her valuable cargo. Her carpenter and armourer, Messrs. Guard and Gallop, had, during the confusion and bustle of the battle before-mentioned, deserted over to the patriot army, and were then permitted to repair on board of one of the patriot vessels of war, from which, by request of Captain Sheffield, they were now received on board of the sloop of war Conway, by order of her worthy captain,* who sent his officer and boat for them, and who, it appears, treated Captain Sheffield, under his misfortune, truly indeed, like a brother in distress. Captain Sheffield, in the hurry of embarking on board of his sloop, when at Valparaiso, to sail for Arauco, had gone on board with no other apparel save the suit he had on, but as soon as at sea, this

* Here the author would respectfully remark, that it is with much regret he finds the name of this very meritorious British commander omitted in the note of record taken while Captain Sheffield was among the living.

gallant officer of the British navy, not only freely tendered, but even insisted, in the warmth of persuasion, on Captain Sheffield's making free use of his wardrobe, as if it was his own; and in addition to his numerous friendly acts of comfort to those bare and distressed American mariners, he urged Captain Sheffield, when they came to part, to take and accept of a sum of money to provide for his and their passage home; saying, he would take no voucher for it, and that if thereafter it should not be perfectly convenient for him to return t, then never to think of it, or let it in the least trouble his mind. Captain Sheffield returned to him his most unfeigned thanks for this very generous tender, and for his many favours and kindness, saying, that the United States' Consul had kindly furnished him with all the pecuniary aid he should require.

The embassy to Arauco of the commander of His Britannic Majesty's sloop, being thus, by the goodness and merit of the admiral, Sir T. M. Hardy, carried into effect, her anchor was weighed, and she returned back to the port of Valparaiso, where her able commander made his report to his senior in the command of the British squadron on this station; when that fatherly United States' Consul, M. Hogan, Esq., joined with Captain Sheffield in presenting their heartfelt thanks to the British commodore, Sir T. M. Hardy, for his benevolent and kind assistance in endeavouring to relieve the unfortunate. Captain Sheffield thereon remarked, in his acknowledgment, that the kind and handsome manner in which these favours had been conferred by the noble admiral, and the generous and courteous commander of His Britannic Majesty's sloop, Conway, would never be erased from his heart and memory. In fact, Captain Sheffield now says, that the doings, acts, and treatment of the admiral to the unfortunate, was praiseworthy beyond expression, or any thing he could say. With many and grateful thanks for the same meritorious acts, &c., as an American citizen, and agent of the Hersilia's voyage, the author closes the narrative, simply remarking, that Captain Sheffield, his officers, and men took passage, and arrived safely at their home in the United States.

APPENDIX.

AMERICAN NATIONAL SOUTH SEA EXPLORING EXPEDITION.

New-York, January 3, 1838.—The author being informed by letters from Washington, that Commodore Thomas Ap C. Jones has resigned the command of the United States' South Sea Exploring Expedition; and also that it was in contemplation to reorganize the expedition, as to the vessels, &c.; and the author having at its first commencement addressed and forwarded to His Excellency, President Jackson, a letter containing his plan and views on the expedition, as to the kind of vessels, &c., which should compose the expedition, to warrant, in his humble opinion, a promise of the greatest benefit and most brilliant result; he therefore felt it now a duty again to communicate the like, by letter, of similar tenor, to His Excellency President Van Buren, and promptly forwarded to his Excellency the following address:—

New-York, December 18th, 1837.

To His Excellency MARTIN VAN BUREN,
President of the United States,
Washington City.

I have respectfully to observe, that, believing it to be the duty of every good citizen, when he has reason to believe his country requires it, to contribute his aid, if ever so small and humble, as well in the aid by light on any measure of government, as otherwise ;—this, with the reported difficulty that appears to have risen on the Exploring Expedition, has caused the idea to come up to my mind, and with the utmost respect, to again lay before the President, in recommendation, (if it is to be reorganized,) my original plan and view, as to what vessels, &c., should best compose an American National Discovery and Exploring Expedition to the South Seas, &c., to warrant the greatest benefit, and give a promise of the most brilliant result in every view, viz.—

In the greatest respectful deference to all others, and their opinions, my practical knowledge would recommend a well constructed and light armed navy-like flag ship, with the most superior comfortable accommodations for all on board, which would cost, say $100,000, with two small proper exploring ships, with similar accommodations, and which two would cost, say $80,000. Those three vessels coming at this sum of $180,000, exclusive of their armament, which government has on hand at their depots, with a complement of not exceeding 275 persons, scientific and all told; would, in my humble opinion, compose the most proper and effective South Sea American National Discovery and Exploring Expedition. And thus, all three sailing alike, would give them great advantage in keeping company, and prevent delay; and such vessels could, in their out fit, receive on board of each all their main wants for a four years' voyage, with the occasional required refreshments that would come convenient in their route, and therefore be dependent on themselves only while on the voyage, (and not on a victualling ship,*) and would be by far the best squadron of vessels for performance in this peculiar service, and to ensure the best promise of constant health to their crews—would also take away all heart-burning from every individual, as to a preference in the vessels to sail in, as the three would be alike comfortable to all. And those would perform the service with the

* Which may cause serious disappointment to all dependent, by being wrecked while on her passage from one rendezvous to another.

greatest despatch and safety, and certainly in much less time than the present prepared expedition possibly could; and it appears to my experience, with that of the economy, of less than a moiety of the amount of its expense; in fact, in every view, does it not appear wise that such a squadron would be the preferable? and surely it would be truly American, and carry thus with it, special national dignity. And as all the now provided articles, provisions, instruments, &c., &c., could be transferred over to them, those three most proper vessels* could be completed, and at anchor off our bat-

* A wise government should never send a vessel to penetrate into the icy regions towards the South Pole, unless she was able to take and had on board at least eighteen months full allowance of fuel and provisions, to the safety of those on board; as when she is advanced into these regions, her scene may, in spite of all human precaution, in an hour's time, be changed from that of a clear sky, and free of ice, to being enveloped in a thick dense fog—and before this clears away, she may get beset, and fast, in a vast field of ice, extending beyond the vision, and thus detained through a long winter, and even the next season in extricating her, to the liberty of proceeding on any desired course. And to send her on this route without being thus wisely provided, would seem to be sporting with valuable lives. Also vessels sent on this service should have two decks, and be of the most expert working, and swiftest sailing vessels. And further, those two smaller vessels are certainly not the safest to explore and survey singly among the islands and natives in the Pacific,

tery by, or on the 4th of July next, at the very farthest, ready for sea at an hour's notice, whenever its gallant commander should receive his orders for sailing, and which date would be a favourable season for it to sail. And on their return, being the swiftest sailing vessels, and first rate sea-boats, would be the very thing for the relief cruising squadron on our coast in relieving the distressed vessels, agreeable to the contemplated bill recently before Congress.

All which is most respectfully submitted, and have the honour to be, with great respect,

The President's

Most ob'd't servant,

EDMUND FANNING.

In answer to which letter, the author, by return mail, received from the honourable secretary of the United States' navy, the following note :—

Navy Department, 22d December, 1837.

Sir,—Your letter to the President of the 18th inst., respecting the South Sea Exploring Ex-

as being not higher, or so high out of water, as the platform of their large double war canoes, will be much more likely to invite attack, war, and massacre.

pedition, has been referred to this department, and shall receive a respectful consideration.

I am with great respect, your ob'd't servant,

M. DICKERSON.

Captain EDMUND FANNING,
New-York.

Finally, in closing, the author would respectfully remark, that the part he has acted, touching on this laudable national enterprise, with the purest intentions and views to serve his country, is herein faithfully recorded ; and he cheerfully leaves it with a generous public, and the candid reader, to judge, and decide, whether he is subject to any blame, as his aid by knowledge in experience of voyaging to those parts, and seas, has never been called into requisition in its preparations ; also to judge if this omission has not been at least unwise touching its organization, delay, or tending to its failure, (which heaven forbid,) should the expedition entirely fail of ever departing from an American port. Let them determine whether he has been treated according to his merits, and patriotic intentions, to serve his country by aid to navigation, commercial trade, the whale and seal fisheries, science, &c., &c., as well as to make it more safe to the voyaging storm suffering mariner, while on his route traversing those seas and oceans. And whether the author has had his merits so awarded in relation to his acts and doings, touching on this national enterprise and subject, by a just and liberal treatment, &c., as to encourage other citizens to appropriate their choicest time in life, in patriotic acts, and researches for the general good and benefit of their country. As the author conceives, if this national expedition be worth any thing to the nation, then he has been very unhandsomely and ungratefully treated, in being kept aside, and not admitted to participate in its fit out, even if no benefit should have been derived thereby.

The author has deemed it but justice due, to thus place on record before the public, and the world, the part he has acted relative to this national project, lest error, and a false view, should hereafter come up into belief, to the injury of a plain voyager, and with all respectful deference, he hopes this will be a satisfactory apology to those highly worthy gentlemen and citizens whose names he has been under the necessity to use in composing this work. He will only respectfully add, that it may be confidently believed, that had such three ships, properly fitted, have departed from our port on this Discovery and Exploring Expedition in due season, under the able talent in our navy, not only a good part of this very laudable service would have now (January 15th, 1838,) been already performed, but, also thus organized, the author could have seemingly pledged his life, to its honourable, brilliant, and beneficial result. Further, to show in evidence the length of time the author's mind and attention has been drawn to such a national enterprise, he would here respectfully remark, that he has the honour still to hold the commission issued and granted to him by President Madison, of date, 17th of March, 1812, as commander of an Exploring and Discovery Expedition to the South Seas, and around the world, consisting of two suitable ships then prepared and fitting out at the port of New-York, for the voyage, which were prevented from sailing on it, by the sudden declaration of war against Great Britain by the United States' Congress, to the great regret and disappointment of the author, as well as to many scientific gentlemen, and worthy patriotic citizens that felt a weighty interest in this laudable and promising enterprise, in which some of the most able nautical and talented mariners had volunteered and engaged. As the history of the rise and proceedings of the present National South Sea Exploring Expedition is herein particularly related, it is left with the candid reader to judge what unseen current, or cause, kept the personal services of the author from being employed in the constructing of the most proper vessels, as well as to the preparations in its fit out; after his long and arduous task in aid to the obtaining of its authorization, and volunteering, by earliest tender to his Excellency the President of the United States, of the author's personal services to its organization, &c., by the patriotic aid of practical knowledge in such long tried experience, which gave so fair a promise of tending so much to the credit of the nation, and to the benefit and advantage of our beloved country. Nevertheless, after all, although the author has had the fortune, and been the means of causing millions to flow into the nation's treasury, by opening and advancing the herein-before mentioned commercial trade to those southern and eastern countries, the South Seas, Pacific, and China, by which it was made unnecessary to take the specie out from ours therefor; yet, he has never received a dollar from government for any personal services. Such has been the return (non-employment) to a citizen who has voluntarily dedicated a life in research and discovery to the benefit of his country. Having, however, before closing the matter of this volume, received information from Washington, that government had it under consideration to make a change of the vessels then prepared for the South Sea Exploring Expedition, by substituting the sloops of war Vincennes and Peacock, with a packet-built ship; he is confident, from personal experience, that sloops of war are not the best, or even well adapted for a flag-ship, or for explorers to such an expedition and service. They can sail around the world, it is true, with the despatch of a vessel of war, by having the attendance of a store-ship, or some like resource to attend to their occasional wants and timely supplies of provisions, fuel, &c., but are certainly not the best adapted vessels for a voyage of discovery and exploration in all climes, latitudes, and seas. The author therefore felt it a duty, and promptly forwarded the following letter to His Excellency the President of the United States.

New-York, February 8th, 1838.

To His Excellency MARTIN VAN BUREN,
President of the United States,
Washington City.

I would respectfully crave once more to address the President on the South Sea Exploring Expedition, as I cannot but consider myself the father of the project in its first start and rise into authorization, and which, to my mind, appears so plain and easy to be carried brilliantly into effect, with the proper vessels, &c.

Being informed from Washington, that government have it under consideration to make a change in the vessels of the expedition, by substituting two sloops of war, the relief, a packet ship, and a schooner, in the room of the frigate and her prepared craft; if this be the fact, with all respectful deference, I should think those more illy adapted to perform this service, than the frigate and her small vessels were. And if the packet ship is intended to accommodate the scientific gentlemen, it is not unwise to separate the main of the scientific corps from an immediate and constant association with its commander.

I therefore, in the utmost respect, beg to submit the following suggestion, viz.—As the Macedonian is prepared, to let her go as the flag-ship, supported by the relief store-ship, and cause to be promptly constructed by the force of our carpenters, &c. here, two small proper ships as the explorers, let those four depart as the squadron; my life on it, those will perform to the honour and credit of the nation, its administration, and the navy.

If desired, the little schooner Active, could be added as a surveying boat, in attendance on the commodore's ship.

With great respect, I have the honour to be,

The President's ob'd't servant,

EDMUND FANNING.

And having voluntarily thus given his aid in the proceedings to this patriotic national enterprise, the author can only say, that ever since the tender of his services, by letter to the President of the United States, which was, it is presumed, the first application, and previous to any appointment being made to the expedition; he has been ever ready, up to the present time, (February 1838,) to give his further aid to this very laudable national project, if it had been called for, and that with a patriotic, honest, and zealous view, to benefit his beloved country and mankind. Nevertheless, thus ended the voluntary exertions of years of toil in the best spirit of good intent of the author, to aid in his best endeavours to effect this really favourite national measure by the most promising fit out to the expedition, &c.

Thus, also perished all the long, sanguine and flattering hopes of the author, on which his heart has so long been set, to a supreme idea of pleasure and gratification, in the hope of seeing this favourite national enterprise sail, and return during his time of life with brilliant success, and honour to the nation, its navy, science, &c., and thereby adding much to the American character. And now, when fate has so singularly and slowly dragged it forward into partial preparation ; still if ever the squadron proceed on its discoveries and explorations, its performance and result are yet wrapt in the darkness of futurity, and to the author most likely ever will be ; as after its being so long suspended on the wings of doubt, must defeat his anxious expectation, as should it now, this day, depart from the shore of America, there is a very small prospect that the author, by his advanced age, would be found among the living on its return.

The author would not have the reader understand by the tenor of his letter, as above to the President, that he would have preferred a frigate to all other vessels as a flag-ship, or to that of a ship built expressly for this particular service and station, which, like the two suggested exploring ships, could receive before sailing all her main wants on board for her voyage, and therefore, not liable to disappointment and delay, by being dependent on a store-ship. But, as the Macedonian had been prepared ready to depart—to prevent any further delay in the sailing of the expedition, he deemed it best to employ her as the flag-ship, as first intended. A sloop of war being not only much smaller, but single decked, is thus by no means well calculated for a flag and home ship to such an expedition. If, at the very first, one of our splendid large packet ships, or a vessel modelled and constructed like them, had been selected or decided on to have been employed as the flag-ship to this uncommon new service, frigate rigged, and lightly, navy-like armed, it would, in the author's humble opinion, have been a wise and good selection.

The author having been honoured in the command of a corvette ship of war of 22 guns, commissioned by the elder President Adams, on an exploring voyage around the world; and important discoveries having been by him made, to much national benefit—and such voyage having been well and safely performed, is it not likely that he should by this, and his many other like voyages, as well as great experience in ship building, be somewhat of a judge, as to what kind of vessels would be the most suitable, and best in promise to perform on a National Discovery and Exploring Expedition, to all seas and climes? As also to the propriety of employing sloops of war on this important national enterprise, either as a flag-ship, or as explorers, or as being the best and driest sea-boats, tending thereby to the comfort and preservation of the health of the crew? In illustration of this, the author would respectfully refer to the circumstances as related of the Peacock sloop of war, when sailing in the mild climate under the fortieth degree of south latitude, where, in Roberts' Embassy, page 30, it is thus remarked:—

"The ship (the Peacock) was at one time rolling her channels in before a strong westerly wind; at another, lying with her broadside deeply submerged by severe squalls from the northwestern quarter, the gun-deck being ankle deep in water, and washing from side to side. *Life lines* were secured from gun to gun to support the constant passing of men fore and aft the deck."

And again, on the adjoining page 31.

"Subsequently, we encountered a very heavy gale, accompanied by a tremendous swell of the ocean; during its violence, a sea of uncommon height struck the ship,* and threw her nearly on her beam ends, and buried the

* This stroke of the sea was, it is presumed, owing to the deficiency of that duck-like buoyancy in the Peacock, by her uncommon and too heavy frame, &c., in her construc-

first three ratlines of the mizen shrouds under water."

The author would most respectfully ask, how could American talent and wisdom deem such vessels the most suitable as flags or explorers, especially to navigate on this new and extraordinary service, and in all climes and latitudes, such as the regions of the icy seas, where much heavier weather, and more violent gales would be expected to be met with, than in the milder latitudes? Having at all times in view, and expectation to perform, and accomplish by American perseverance, fortitude, and talent, beyond what has been heretofore performed by all other navigators, since the days of Columbus, and thereby to advance the American character; he would inquire, are such vessels (sloops of war,) to be selected, preferred, and chosen, to thus perform on this new and important service; and that too, after building three other vessels expressly for it, which, after trial, are found unfit. Alas! my country; has all thy wisdom and Yankee '*cuteness* of character flown to the winds.

The following extract of a letter to the Hon.

tion when rebuilt, which deadened her buoyant life, and thereby prevented her prompt rise over the giant sea, like a first rate sea-boat.

John Forsyth, secretary of state for the United States, will give the author's view as to the route, performances, &c., expected, relative to the expedition. As also the difference between a mere surveying expedition; and that of a magnificent National Discovery and Exploring Expedition.

(EXTRACT.)

New-York, February 24th, 1838.

Sir,—Therein I respectfully would state, it appears that the Exploring Expedition is to spend the main part of its time from the 20th degree of north latitude to the south, in *surveying* the islands, &c. in the Pacific.* This employment would be time well used, to be sure, whenever the squadron were waiting for the season to come around favourable to proceed into a higher latitude, or, if it was intended to be a mere surveying expedition.

* In all deference, I should think, to perform any thing like a correct survey of all the islands, reefs, &c., lying in the Pacific, between the tropics, it would give constant and active employment to ten sail, for at least ten years, to well accomplish. This, a Discovery and Exploring Expedition could effect, as only touching on the most prominent objects on their route, and then only as far as time would conveniently admit of.

But with all respectful deference, relative to its object, I have ever been in the belief, it had in view a more dignified, magnanimous, and important service and performance as a National Discovery and Exploring Expedition, viz.—That its gallant commander would, as far as possible, in the Northern, as well as in the Southern Pacific, and also in other oceans, cause all unexplored seas, and lands, to be explored, the eastern coast of Asia, the extensive islands north of Japan, so little known, &c.; and may I respectfully suggest, should a person be on board the flag-ship, having in charge a letter or friendly communication from the President of the United States of America, to the Emperor of Japan;* on that ship's visiting one of his ports, with the intention of a trial to obtain the freedom of a port, in one of the numerous harbours on the eastern coast of Japan, to which our whale ships might be permitted to resort to, when in want of refreshments, or in case of repairing damage met with in that sea; this would be highly important and beneficial accommodation to those whale ships, and

* Our late venerable President Jackson has thus obtained a friendly understanding with the King of Siam, the great lord and worshipper of the white elephant, and other oriental nabobs, and why may not the like succeed with the Emperor of Japan?—it certainly cannot be known until tried.

the enterprising citizens employed on board, in that very valuable fishery. And should this be acceded to, and accomplished, who can tell but what it might be the means of opening the gate to an extensive advantageous commercial trade hereafter with that empire.

I have the honour to be, dear sir,

Very respectfully,

Your ob'd't servant,

EDMUND FANNING.

Herewith the reader has the official Report of the honourable secretary of the navy, in answer to a resolution of the honourable the House of Representatives of the American Congress, relating to the National South Sea Exploring Expedition.

25th Congress, 2d Session. [Doc. No. 147.] Ho. of Reps. Executive.

EXPLORING EXPEDITION.

MESSAGE

FROM

THE PRESIDENT OF THE UNITED STATES,

TRANSMITTING

The information required by a resolution of the House of Representatives of 7th December last, in relation to the Delay in the Outfit, &c., for the Exploring Expedition.

February 7, 1838.
Read, and laid upon the table.

Washington City, *February* 5, 1838.

Sir: I have the honour to transmit to you a report from the Secretary of the Navy, prepared in obedience to a resolution of the House of Representatives of the 7th December last, requiring information as to the causes which have delayed the outfit and preparation of the South Sea Surveying and Exploring Expedition.

M. VAN BUREN.

To the Hon. James K. Polk,
Speaker of the Ho. of Reps.

NAVY DEPARTMENT, *February* 5, 1838.

SIR: I have the honour to transmit to you a report, in obedience to the resolution of the House of Representatives of the 7th December last, in relation to the delay of the sailing of the Exploring Expedition.

I am, very respectfully,

Your obedient servant.

M. DICKERSON.

To the PRESIDENT *of the United States.*

NAVY DEPARTMENT, *February* 5, 1838.

SIR: In obedience to a resolution of the House of Representatives of the 7th December last, calling for the causes which have delayed the outfit and preparation of the South Sea Surveying and Exploring Expedition, required by the act of Congress of May, 1836, making appropriations for the naval service; and copies of all letters, documents, and communications, which have passed between the Secretary of the Navy, the Commissioners of the Navy Board, the officer appointed to the chief command, and of all other officers or persons, relative to all matters connected with the preparation, outfit, and sailing of the said expedition, and the causes which now delay its sailing; I beg leave to state that, in my report of the 2d of December last, I gave a brief detail of the circumstances which had caused the delay of the sailing of this expedition up to that time, when I believed that it was about to leave our coast. The vessels of the squadron were at the harbour of New York, nearly ready for sea; the scientific corps had been directed to report to the commander, and had done so, and were ready to embark. My sailing instructions were given as early as the 10th of November; the seamen, ordinary seamen, marines, and boys, had re-entered, and received their bounty, in whole or in part, to the amount of three months' pay; when, on being permitted to go on shore, they deserted, to the number of one hundred and fifty-five; and Commodore Jones, harassed with the trouble and labour of preparing his vessels for sea, found his health so entirely destroyed that he could not, either in justice to himself or to the country, longer continue in command of the squadron. He transmitted the copy of a letter from Dr. R. Ticknor, fleet surgeon of the expedition, dated at New York, November 30, 1837, stating that the commodore's health had been in a bad state for some time; that, from the violent cough under which he was suffering, from the bloody expectoration and soreness in the chest, it was evident that the lungs were diseased to such a degree as to demand serious attention; and that, considering his predisposition to pulmonary disease, and the unfavourable influence of the climate of that place upon such predisposition, it was his opinion that a change of climate was the only measure from which the desired benefit could be obtained. He therefore strongly advised the commodore to leave that climate, and go to his residence in Virginia, as soon as the state of his health and the weather would permit.

Under these circumstances, the commodore's request to be relieved from the command of the squadron was immediately granted; although this measure could not fail to be attended with the most embarrassing circumstances, as it respected the sailing of the squadron. Great difficulty was apprehended in finding a successor to Commodore Jones, able and willing to take the command of the squadron, as it had been organized, or to remodel the same. All these difficulties have been fully realized. The command has been offered to three distinguished officers, who have declined it; a fourth has been ordered, who will not be permitted to decline, under whom the squadron will be reorganized on a reduced scale, and through whose agency there is a fair prospect of realizing the important objects of the expedition.

I have endeavoured to lay before Congress the important facts connected with the fitting out of this expedition in my annual report of the 3d of December, 1836; in my letter of the 6th of February last, in answer to a call of the House of Representatives for information as to the progress made with regard to the Exploring Expedition, (Doc. No. 138;) in my letter of the 12th of October last, in answer to a call of the House of Representatives in relation to the detention of the sailing of the Exploring squadron, (Doc. No. 50;) and in my last annual report of the 2d of December last. To these documents I beg leave to refer as explanatory of the present report. I will now attempt to restate the leading facts contained in those documents, with such remarks and additional information as the present resolution seems to require.

In the act of the 14th of May, 1836, making appropriations for the naval service, it was provided that the President of the United States be authorized to send out a Surveying and Exploring Expedition to the Pacific Ocean and South Seas; and for that purpose to employ a sloop of war, and to purchase or provide such other smaller vessels as might be proper and necessary to render such expedition efficient and useful; for which the sum of one hundred and fifty thousand dollars was appropriated: and, in addition thereto, if necessary, the President was authorized to use other means in the control of the Navy Department, not exceeding one hundred and fifty thousand dollars, for the objects required.

It is evident that a sloop of war, a brig, and a schooner, was as large a force as it was the intention of Congress to employ on this expedition. Had this plan been adopted, the expedition, with a small scientific corps, and such instruments and books as were to be procured in the country, might have sailed before the meeting of Congress of that year; although this would have interfered with other branches of the naval service, then requiring the immediate attention of the Navy Department.

Captain Thomas Ap Catesby Jones was se lected as the commander of the expedition. The confidence placed in this officer, which led to his appointment to this important trust, induced the President to rely upon his opinion as to the proper force to be employed.

He was of the opinion that one frigate of the second class, one store-ship, two barques or brigs, and one schooner, were indispensably necessary to the success of the enterprize. In accordance with which opinion, measures were taken for preparing the vessels and fitting out the expedition. The frigate Macedonian and store-ship Relief were upon the stocks at the time this measure was adopted, and were ordered to be finished without delay, and the three other vessels were ordered to be built—the whole under the immediate superintendence of Commodore Jones, who was authorized to visit, as often as he should think proper, the different navy yards of Boston, New-York, Philadelphia, and Norfolk, for the purpose of giving such directions and instructions as he might deem necessary.

As this great national enterprise would cost more for its outfit than the whole sum appropriated for the expedition, it was evident that it could not leave our coast until further appropriations should be made.

This afforded an opportunity of sending to Europe for books and instruments for the scientific corps to be attached to the squadron; and rendered it proper to increase the proposed number for such corps, so as to bear a just proportion to the great scale of the expedition.

Lieutenant Wilkes, of the navy, was sent to Europe, with ample funds, to procure the necessary books and instruments, and embarked at New-York on the 8th of August, 1836.

As at this time it was necessary to fit out a squadron for the Pacific, another for the coast of Brazil, and to add to our squadron in the West Indies, it was evident that great difficulty would take place in recruiting seamen for the Exploring Expedition. This difficulty was fully understood and stated; but Commodore Jones gave assurances that, should he be authorized to recruit seamen for this particular service, under his own superintendence, and with the aid of such officers as he should designate, he would have a sufficient number of seamen recruited before the ships of the squadron could be prepared.

This proposition was assented to, although this mode of recruiting was considered extremely detrimental to the service. This measure, as was apprehended, made it necessary to adopt the same mode of recruiting for the Brazilian and Pacific squadrons, all interfering with each other; and the consequence was, that on the first of February last, no more than two hundred and forty-eight seamen, ordinary seamen, and boys, had been recruited for the expedition—more than enough, it is true, for the expedition intended by Congress, but not half enough for the squadron of Commodore Jones, which required crews, officers included, amounting to six hundred and three men, exclusive of the scientific corps.

At the different navy yards every effort was made to complete, agreeably to the suggestions and instructions of Commodore Jones, the vessels of this squadron, to wit: the frigate Macedonian, the store-ship Relief, of 460 tons, the barques Pioneer and Consort, of 230 tons each, and the schooner Pilot, of 114 tons. The Relief was launched on the 14th of September, 1836; the Pioneer on the 26th, and the Consort on the 29th of October; the Pilot about the same time, and the frigate Macedonian on the 1st of November. The barques and schooner, with the store-ship, were equipped and sent round to Norfolk, from which harbour they might sail at any season of the year.

Before this time, a difficulty had occurred as to the appointment of two officers to the command of two of the smaller vessels, which, although it occasioned no delay in the sailing of the squadron, had an unfavourable effect upon the preparations for the expedition.

It was my wish to employ such officers of the navy as were distinguished for science, in this expedition, as far as this could conveniently be done; and to employ but a small number of scientific gentlemen not belonging to the navy. Upon such an arrangement I believed the ultimate success of the expedition was to depend, and have not changed that opinion.

Lieutenant Slidell, distinguished for his scientific attainments and elegant literature, seemed peculiarly well qualified to take a place in the expedition; I, therefore, proposed to order him to the command of one of the smaller vessels of the squadron, and to charge him with the duty of writing a history of the voyage.

To this Commodore Jones, after taking time for inquiry and consideration, objected in a written communication. This I received and considered; for the rule I had adopted as to this expedition was, not only to permit Commodore Jones to select his officers, such as commanders of squadrons are usually permitted to select, but, of those to be selected by this Department, not to appoint any against whom he might have well-founded objections; and such were the instructions to me from the President.

The objections to Lieutenant Slidell appeared to me not only unfounded, but unjust to the professional character and standing of that officer. As he requested a copy of those objections, which were made a matter of record in this Department, it was, with the assent of Commodore Jones communicated to him; and he was left to answer the allegations which had been made against him.

I proposed to order Lieutenant Wilkes to the command of the schooner, from a belief that his knowledge in mathematics and astronomy would be of great service to the expedition;

with a view to which, he had been selected to go to Europe for instruments and books, as before stated. To him also, Commodore Jones objected in a written communication. His objections appeared to me not to be well founded; I, however, did not order either of these officers, but reserved the subject for the consideration of the President, who was then absent from the seat of government. On his return, it was laid before him, and he decided in favour of ordering those officers, as I had proposed. As, however, the correspondence between Lieutenant Slidell and Commodore Jones was such as to leave no hope that there could be any harmony of action between them, which might be attended with consequences unfavourable to the success of the expedition; and as the objections made against Lieutenant Wilkes, who had not yet returned from Europe, were such as to leave no doubt in my mind that he would consider it an act of injustice, under the circumstances of the case, to be ordered in this service, I came to the conclusion that for the interest of the expedition it was better that neither of them should be ordered. I informed Commodore Jones that they would not be ordered, and requested him to name the officers he wished.

After this, I made no further attempts to secure for this expedition the services of officers of science; and from that time there has been a great reluctance on the part of officers to to serve in the expedition, as is evident from the great number ordered, who, upon their earnest solicitation, have been excused; a list of whom is annexed to this report.

Soon after this, (on the 4th of December,) Congress met. At this time Lieutenant Wilkes had not returned to the United States with the instruments and books, although daily expected. The necessary recruits of seamen had not been obtained, and the appropriation of three hundred thousand dollars was nearly exhausted. The squadron could not sail upon the extensive scale adopted, until further appropriaticns should be made; and these were not made until the 3d of March last. In the mean time, it was not considered certain that Congress would, by their appropriations, authorize the sending out a larger squadron than they had intended by the act of May, 1836.

In my annual report of the 3d of December, 1836, I submitted estimates of appropriations required for the expedition, to consist of one frigate, one store-ship, two barques, and one schooner; and on the 6th of February last, I made, as before stated, a report in answer to a resolution of the House of Reprcsentatives, in relation to the progress made in fitting out the

Exploring Expedition, in which these estimates were fully explained.

By these reports it appears that the appropriation of three hundred thousand dollars had been expended, and that the annual expense for the five vessels of the squadron, with pay and provisions for the scientific corps, would amount to $346,431, which, for three years, the proposed duration of the cruise, would amount to $1,039,293.

Although the appropriation for the payment of the scientific corps had not been made, yet their appointment was urged on the ground that it was important to the gentlemen to be selected, to know it as long beforehand as possible, to enable them to arrange their business for an absence of three years: and on the 28th of December, 1836, the larger part of them were appointed, on liberal salaries, to commence when their services should be required; upon which condition, they accepted their appointment.

On the 30th of March last Lieutenant Tattnall returned from a cruise to the coast of Mexico, which he had made as commander of the Pioneer; and he reported so unfavourably of the sailing of this vessel, that it was deemed proper that her condition should be fully examined into, as well as that of the brig Consort and schooner Pilot, which, in point of sailing, had not been considered equal to the Pioneer.

The necessary arrangements for such an examination were made; and on the 10th of April Commodore Jones was informed that the Commissioners of the Navy, with the chief naval constructor and the naval architect at Norfolk, were ready to proceed to the performance of this duty; and he was requested to join them, which he did.

On the 26th of that month, at his own suggestion, he was instructed to make an experimental cruise with the Relief, Pioneer, Consort and Pilot, for the purpose of making a full trial of their sailing qualities, and was directed to return to Norfolk in twenty days after sailing. On his return from this cruise, he reported favourably of the sailing of these vessels; but, in other respects, his report might be considered as unfavourable, inasmuch as he recommended that the barques and schooner should go into dry dock for the purpose of examination, and such alterations as a board of officers appointed for that purpose should recommend. This could not fail to add to the delay which had already taken place, as the ship of the line Delaware was then in dock, and could not be immediately removed.

Lieutenant Tattnall, after this experimental cruise, still entertained the most unfavourable opinion of the sailing qualities of these vessels, and asked to be relieved from the command of the Pioneer.

As soon as the Delaware could be removed, Commodore Warrington, on the 30th of May, was directed to prepare the Pioneer, Consort, and Pilot, for going into dock. On the 8th of June, a board of five officers (Commodores Chauncey, Morris, Warrington, Patterson, and Wadsworth,) was ordered to make an examination of the condition of those vessels; which seemed the more necessary, inasmuch as Commodore Jones had demanded another schooner to be added to his squadron; without which he could not consider the expedition complete or efficient.

The board was instructed to inquire whether the squadron might not be reduced in number of vessels and men, with advantage to the country, and without prejudice to the success of the expedition.

This inquiry was rendered proper in consequence of the great difficulty of procuring the necessary funds during the suspension of specie payments, which had not been foreseen when the last appropriations were made, and because it would be in accordance with the original intentions of Congress in fitting out the expedition. It was thought that, should a part of the vessels be found unfit for this service, it would be better that the squadron should sail with a reduced force, than suffer the delay of preparing other vessels. On the 17th of June Commodore Jones reported that the requisite number of seamen had been recruited.

On the 12th of July, the board reported that the occupation of the dock at Gosport, and the employment of some of the members of the board, prevented a meeting until the 30th June; that the barques and schooner were put into dock and examined; and certain alterations recommended, which could soon be completed, by which the vessels might be made to answer the purpose proposed *sufficiently well to justify their employment.*

The board say that had they been called upon, before any preparations had been made, to state the number and character of the vessels which, in their opinion, would be best calculated to secure the attainment of the proposed objects, they certainly would not have recommended those which have been prepared.

They were of opinion that a smaller number of vessels would have answered the purposes; yet, from a consideration of the expense incurred, the time spent in preparing the force, and other circumstances, which they enumerate, and as the officer selected to command the expedition was satisfied with the vessels, they came to the conclusion that no reduction could be made in their amount at this late period, without prejudice to the success of the expedition. They, however, recommended a reduction of the number of officers and men to about five hundred, exclusive of the scientific corps. To this reduction Commodore Jones strenuously objected, and he was permitted to retain his full force of 603 officers and men.

The alterations recommended in the vessels were made with all the despatch that the means at the disposal of Commodore Warrington would permit. But, before they could be completed, Commodore Jones discovered that the cooking galleys which had been ordered to be put on board his vessels, by his direction, for burning anthracite coal, would not answer the purpose proposed; and on the 1st of August he requested that new galleys should be furnished, to be substituted for those found to be useless. This was a new cause of delay. Orders were immediately given for constructing the new galleys wanted. They were made without delay, at the navy yard at Washington, under the direction of Commodore Patterson, and the last of them sent to Norfolk on the 6th of October.

As I believed the schooner Pilot, notwithstanding the alterations made in her, could not be safely employed in this expedition, I gave Commodore Jones the privilege of purchasing another schooner, to be substituted for this. In consequence of which, on the 8th of September, he purchased the schooner Clara, now called the Active, for eight thousand dollars; upon which he was authorized to put such repairs and improvements as he might think necessary, at the navy yard at New-York; and which he has done at a much greater expense than the original cost of the vessel.

On the 26th of September I had issued orders to Commodore Jones to proceed with his squadron from Norfolk to New-York, as soon as the vessels could be prepared for removal. He sailed from Norfolk on the 12th of October, and arrived four days afterwards at New-York.

Before leaving Norfolk, Commodore Jones issued a general order, which gives a most flattering account of the condition of the squadron, leaving no doubt that the expedition would be under sail, in a few days, for the southern hemisphere.

The reasons alleged by Commodore Jones for wishing to remove the squadron to New-

York were, that the stores might be completed, and such apparatus procured for heating the vessels as might be necessary for the health and comfort of the crews in high latitudes ; all which, it was believed, could be completed in a few days.

Wishing to hasten the departure of the squadron, I instructed the gentlemen of the scientific corps, to report to Commodore Jones without delay, although he had not informed me that the vessels were ready for their reception, but I inferred this from the general order, and it was important that their books, instruments, and furniture should be arranged while the preparations for the vessels were advancing. Although the gentlemen of the scientific corps could not, with propriety, be instructed to report to the commander of the expedition before the vessels were in a situation to receive them, yet they were put upon pay from the 4th of July last, and were on duty in preparing books, instruments, and materials, necessary for their labours on the expedition. Fearing that there might be some difficulty as to accommodations for this corps, and the various articles they might think it necessary to carry with them, I requested Commodore Jones, if his convenience would permit, to meet a large portion of them assembled at Philadelphia, for the purpose of having with them a free conference and perfect understanding as to these points. This meeting took place in July, and such arrangements were made as I understood to be perfectly satisfactory to Commodore Jones and to the gentlemen of the scientific corps.

This arrangement, however, seems to have had no beneficial effect; for the instruments, books, furniture, and articles of various kinds, required by these gentlemen for the expedition, are greater in bulk than can be provided for in all the ships of the squadron.

To prevent a loss of time, I authorized several gentlemen of this corps to purchase such books, instruments, and materials as were necessary, and for which previous requisitions could not conveniently be made; and for a like reason, I placed five thousand dollars in the hands of Commodore Jones, to be disposed of for such articles as he might think necessary; and twelve thousand dollars were lodged with his purser, subject to his drafts for a like purpose. These were variations from the regulations governing expenditures of the navy, but appeared to me to be justified by the circumstances of the case. On the 3d of November Commodore Jones was informed that the chronometers for the squadron were ready for delivery at the depot at Washington, and he was requested to send two competent officers to take charge of them; and on the 16th of the month, twenty-five chronometers, in good order, were delivered to the officers sent for them.

On the 10th of November my sailing instructions had been sent to Commodore Jones, to be carried into effect as soon as his vessels should, in all respects, be ready for sea.

At this time I was not aware of the extent of work to be done upon the vessels after their arrival at New-York; which required more than two months to complete.

This was an unexpected cause of delay. I had given instructions for re-entering the seamen, landsmen, and boys for this expedition, and to give them a bounty equal to three months' pay, which was paid to them, in whole or in part, about the 1st of November; soon after which, one hundred and fifty-five of them who had liberty to go on shore deserted.

This was an unexpected and extremely embarrassing cause of delay; but the most serious cause of delay is, the withdrawal of Commodore Jones from the command of the squadron when it was so nearly prepared for sea.

It was apprehended that there would be a great difficulty in finding an officer able and willing to take the command of this squadron, in the condition in which it had been left by Commodore Jones. It was proposed to Captain Shubrick to take the command, but he objected to the frigate as too large a vessel for this service, and to the brigs Pioneer and Consort, as altogether unfit for it; and not being satisfied with the number of vessels, or the organization of the squadron, he declined the command. The great confidence placed in this officer seemed to require that the validity of his opinions should be fully examined.

A board, consisting of Commodore Hull, Commodore Biddle, and Commander Aulick, was appointed by a letter of the 12th of December, stating that doubts having been entertained both with regard to the fitness of some of the vessels of the exploring squadron for the service on which they were to be employed, and to the extent of force, number, and size of the vessels, the whole subject was referred to a board of experienced officers, in June last, to consider and report upon the same: that, after personal examination and careful investigation, the board reported, that if the matter had been submitted to them originally, they would not have recommended either the extent, size, or composition of the force of the vessels proposed to be employed; but that, taking into consideration the delay that would attend a change in these particulars at that period, and that the commanding officer was satisfied with the number, size and qualities of the vessels, they recommended no change of the vessels, but certain alterations in a part of them, which could soon be made: and that the withdrawal of one commander, and the appointment of another, to this expedition, must necessarily be attended with some delay; and presented the case referred to the board in June last, under circumstances differing from those on which their report was grounded: that the President had, in consequence, determined to avail himself of the aid of the professional advice of the board now appointed, as to the number, size, and equipments of the vessels best calculated to succeed in surveying and exploring operations among the islands of the South Pacific ocean, and in high latitudes of the South seas; and as to the best means of fitting out the same: for the consideration of which subjects, they were required to meet at Washington, which they did on the 19th of December. On the 25th of that month they reported, that to carry into effect the expedition authorized by the act of Congress of the 14th of May, 1836, there will be required, in their opinion, four vessels. "First, a sloop of war of the second class. To fit a sloop of war for this service, it is recommended that her rigging, spars, and sails, be reduced; that in the place of her regular armament, there be substituted an armament of lighter calibre, and fewer in number; and that the established complement of officers and men be diminished, so that the whole number on board shall be about one hundred and thirty. As it may be presumed that the commander of the expedition, in the event of a war during its absence, will be instructed to abstain from all acts of hostility, the military equipments, in the opinion of the board, need not exceed the wants of a vessel employed among the islands of the Pacific. Second: Two ships or barques, of 300 or 350 tons each, of substantial construction, to mount six light guns, to have sixty or seventy men each, including officers; the spars and sails of both vessels to be of equal dimensions, so as to serve alike for either of them. Third: A store-ship of about 450 tons, mounting four light guns, and having fifty or sixty men, officers included. For surveying purposes among the islands, it is recommended that the frames and other materials for one or two decked boats of fifteen or twenty tons, to be put together when wanted, be furnished to the expedition."

The reduction and alteration of the squadron recommended by this board being approved, the command of the expedition was offered to Captain Kearney, who examined the condition of the squadron at New-York. He was not satisfied with the arrangements proposed, and declined the command.

It was then offered to Captain Perry, who, from the situation of his private concerns, felt compelled to decline the command, which, under other circumstances, he would gladly have accepted.

Captain Gregory has now been ordered to the command, and it is confidently hoped that the squadron may sail in a short time, upon the reduced scale recommended by the late board. Some weeks, however, will be required to enable the new commander to re-organize the squadron, and to fit it for service. To send him off without affording him the opportunity of doing this, would be as unjust to him, as hazardous to the success of the expedition.

As the vessels, with their crews, had remained a long time unemployed in the harbour of New-York, it was deemed proper to send out a part of them (the two brigs and schooner) upon a short experimental cruise, charged with the duty of affording relief, under a late act of Congress, to vessels in distress approaching our coast, and which will not retard the sailing of the squadron.

It is believed there can be no impropriety in ordering the seamen engaged for the South Sea Exploring Expedition upon this experimental cruise, and of requiring of them, while upon the same, the duties proposed; although a condition of their re-entering for this expedition was that they should not be "subject to be transferred to the general or any other branch of the naval service of the United States;" a condition that, in its consequences, may be found to be very inconvenient.

The changing of the plan of a small expedition, intended by Congress, to that of the very large one adopted, will account for all the delay that took place until the next meeting of Congress. The difficulty of recruiting seamen, and the want of increased appropriations for the extended plan of the expedition till the 3d of March last, will account for the delay until that time. The unfortunate condition of the vessels built expressly for the expedition; the time necessarily spent in examining and altering them; the introduction of a new kind of cooking galleys for burning anthracite coal, which were found not to answer the purpose proposed, even if anthracite coal had been a fuel easily procured in the Southern regions to be visited by the exploring squadron; the time necessary for constructing new galleys, after they were required in August last; the removal of the squadron to New-York; the desertion of a large portion of the crews; the ill-health, and consequent relief, of Commodore Jones from the command of the squadron; and the fact that the vessels, after their arrival at New-York, required preparations that could not be completed before the 20th of December last, will account for the delay until that time. The difficulty of finding a new commander, and of reorganizing the expedition, has caused the delay since, and must necessarily cause a further delay for a few weeks.

The extraordinary character of the service on this expedition, differing essentially from the duties usually required of the navy, and the preparations for the squadron, so different from those usually required for squadrons on foreign stations, and the power given to Commodore Jones to superintend the preparation of these vessels, have rendered a departure, in some instances, necessary from the regulations of the navy; and the opinions of Commodore Jones, and some of the officers acting under him, as to the observance of regulations deemed necessary by this Department and the Navy Board, have been attended with great inconvenience, as will appear by the correspondence called for by this resolution; copies of which will be transmitted, as soon as the same can be prepared, to be annexed to this report.

I regret that these copies have not been completed; but, from their great extent, and the mass of business pressing upon the clerks of the Department, this has been impossible, without omitting to perform the daily and indispensable business of this office. The copying will be urged with as much despatch as possible; extra clerks have been employed for the purpose; but some weeks must necessarily elapse before the whole can be completed.

I have the honour to be,
Very respectfully,
Your obedient servant,
MAHLON DICKERSON.

To the PRESIDENT *of the United States.*

List of Officers who have been ordered to the Exploring Expedition, and have been excused.

Assistant Surgeon,	James C. Palmer.
Lieutenant,	Josiah Tattnall.
Passed Midshipman,	David D. Porter.
Do	Robert F. Pinkney.
Do	Charles W. Morris.
Do	Thornton A. Jenkins.
Do	Oliver Todd.
Lieutenant,	Henry W. Morris.
Midshipman,	Nathan Barnes.
Lieutenant,	Jacob Crowninshield.
Acting Midshipman,	Henry Rolands.
Lieutenant,	William L. Hudson.
Do	John Rudd.
Surgeon,	William Whelan.
Passed Assistant Surgeon,	A. G. Gambrill.
Passed Midshipman,	E. W. Stull.
Midshipman,	Thomas H. Patterson,
Passed Assistant Surgeon,	Samuel C. Laurason.
Do	John C. Spencer.
Assistant Surgeon,	John Messersmith.
Passed Midshipman,	Richard C. Cagdel.
Lieutenant,	Guert Gansevoort.
Passed Midshipman,	M. G. L. Claiborne.

EXPLORING EXPEDITION.

EXTRACT FROM REMARKS OF MR. CRARY, OF MICHIGAN,

In the House of Representatives, U. S. Congress, April 10th, 1838,

On the motion to reduce the amount of the Appropriation for the Naval Service, for the purpose of putting an end to the South Sea Exploring Expedition.

Mr. Crary said he did not know what could be the object of the gentleman from Virginia (Mr. Mercer) in bringing the character of Commodore Jones into this discussion. From the correspondence between that officer and the Navy Department, every gentleman in the House would form his own opinion.

The gentleman from Virginia might come to one conclusion, and Mr. C. to a very different one. No one had yet attacked the character of Commodore Jones; but if the matter of eulogy was to be carried any farther, there were those who would attack it. Mr. C. was of the number; but in so doing, he had no wish to take from Commodore Jones any of the laurels he had won for past services. He could join in praise of them with as much good will as the gentleman from Virginia.

Mr. C. said that the law of 1836 declared the object of this expedition. It was to visit the Pacific Ocean and the South Seas, and when there, it was to be employed in surveying and exploring. It was advocated by the gentleman from Massachusetts, (Mr. Reed,) on the ground of the immense amount of our commerce in those seas. It was said by that gentleman, and another gentleman from the same state, (Mr. Phillips,) that we had constantly employed there some four hundred and fifty vessels in the whale fishery; that this fleet was manned by upwards of ten thousand men, and cost, with their outfit, about twelve millions of dollars, and were estimated to be worth, when their voyages were completed, twenty millions of dollars. This expedition was designed to aid this commerce, by procuring regular maps and charts of those regions; by ascertaining the character of the tides, currents, and dangerous reefs; by establishing permanent relations with places where our trade was now limited and uncertain; by seeking for, and restoring to their homes and families, those American seamen who had been unfortunately left or cast away upon shores inhabited by a race of savages; and, incidental to all these objects, it was expected that some attention would be paid to the great cause of natural history and science generally.

After much discussion, the advocates of the measure succeeded in convincing the House of its importance. The Executive was authorized to send out "a sloop of war and such other smaller vessels as might be necessary and proper, to render the expedition efficient and useful." President Jackson, in consequence of the past conduct of Captain Jones, called him to the command. The conduct of this officer from that time plainly manifested that his object was to make this a great and magnificent expedition, such as should secure to him lasting renown, and give him, not only a great and dazzling name among his own countrymen, but with the whole civilized world. He looked for his recompense in a wreath of amaranth. Had he confined his views simply to the objects proposed by the House, the squadron might have been at sea long ago. But this would not satisfy his ambition and his vanity. He must have a body guard of scientific men from all "of the most celebrated institutions of the country," to catch birds and flies, toads and fishes. This was all very pretty. There were men in the country who would be delighted with an account of the butterflies that sip the nectar of the flowers that spring up on coral rocks, or of the plumage of a bird that spreads its wings over a far off sea. It was very well to take advantage of so favourable an opportunity to augment the stores of science, but that object should have been only incidental and subordinate to the great purpose of the squadron, which was that of surveying and exploring in the latitudes of an almost unknown sea.

Mr. C. said that he was not originally in favour of this expedition, because he thought we had other and more important objects to attend to nearer home. Said that the blame for the delay of sailing lay between the Secretary of the Navy and Commodore Jones. For his own part, he believed the fault was chargeable on both. Sure he was that Commodore Jones had given the expedition a too scientific character.

(Mr. Mercer here interposed, and said that Commodore Jones had no more to do in fixing the scientific character of the expedition than the gentleman from Michigan.)

Mr. C. resumed, and reminded the gentleman from Virginia, and the House, that Commodore Jones had made it a *sine qua non* that no one of the commanders of the smaller vessels should have a scientific duty assigned to him. As early as the fall of 1836, the Commodore threatened to resign, because the Secretary of the Navy intimated an intention to appoint Lieutenant Slidell to command, and at the same time confer on him the office of historiographer. At a later period, he had been greatly outraged in his feelings because Lieutenant Glynn was offered, and accepted, the appointment of geographer and hydrographer.

(Mr. Mercer here again insisted that the enlargement of the objects of the expedition had not, in any sense, been the act of Commodore Jones.)

Mr. C. would not say that the Commodore had been the cause of the change, but such was his opinion. It was certain that it was made to conform to the views expressed by him in a letter to Mr. Reynolds, written when the expedition was under consideration in this House. There was a wonderful similarity between the views expressed in that letter, and those which had influence in getting up the squadron.

It had been said that the commander of the squadron was not chargeable with the defective construction of the smaller vessels. This fault had been very unjustly ascribed to the chief naval constructor.

This officer acted under special instructions

and he prepared his draughts accordingly. Mr. C. did not know who gave these instructions, but he presumed they came from Commodore Jones, as it was an order of the Department that his wishes should be consulted, and his suggestions adopted, in every thing pertaining to the construction, arrangement, armament, and equipment of the vessels, as far as circumstances would permit. Mr. C. believed that it was a matter of record that the two brigs and the schooner were planned agreeably to the suggestions, and built under the superintendence of Commodore Jones. At any rate, he had exhibited as strong an affection for them as though they were his own children. He had laboured in season and out of season, to convince the public that they were well adapted to the service in which they were to be employed. He had forced Lieutenant Tatnall to tender his resignation of the command of the Pioneer, in consequence of his having expressed the opinion, formed by a cruise among the reefs and currents of the Gulf of Mexico, that she "steered badly when sailing over six knots," and was unable "to claw off a lee shore in a short head sea." The sailing qualities of these bantlings of the commodore had been tested during the past winter. The two brigs had formed a part of our coast squadron.

The Pioneer got ashore in the sound, and had a number of her men severely frost-bitten. The Consort returned to port, after a cruise of fifteen days, with a loss of her main-yard, top-gallant-mast, and one man killed, who was thrown upon deck by her breaching-to against her helm. Lieutenant Glynn, a gallant officer, a good seaman, and a man of science, was in command of her, and in his report of the cruise to Commodore Ridgely he says:

"Off the wind with any sea on, the Consort is dangerous, and should never be allowed to go over six knots; at seven knots she became unmanageable, and, I think, could not possibly be made to go eight knots while drawing more than twelve feet water: for her short and full water lines, particularly abaft, make so much wake, that from five knots and upwards the rudder plays in more or less dead water, and thus its influence is diminishing till it ceases to be the principal directing power. Her full of the body and low transom afford a fair hold for a sea coming up with her, while her want of length allows her to be swung round as upon a pivot. In scudding, therefore, long before she had attained a velocity sufficient to diminish perceptibly the violence of the following sea, she would be breached-to, or brought by the lee. * * * * * *

"It would be impossible to drag her off a lee shore if there was any thing of a sea on. While lying-to on the 29th of January, she pitched every thing beyond the knight-heads under water, and carried away the foretop-gallant mast. Any attempt at that time to force the vessel through the water by carrying the square-sails, must soon have terminated in the loss of her masts; and I was quite satisfied if she was ever fairly caught within twenty miles of a lee shore in a gale of half as many hours duration, she must have been inevitably wrecked."

And yet these are the vessels that were to explore and survey the islands and reefs of the Pacific, and go among the icebergs of the South Seas! The first severe gale of wind when off a lee shore would have sent them to destruction. No man can blame sailors for running away from such vessels, or from a commander who could speak in praise of their excellent qualities. He thought the expedition ought to have been at sea a year ago. The Secretary of the Navy, or Commodore Jones, was answerable for the delay. If the former had done his duty, he ought to call the latter to a strict account; but if the Secretary was in fault, he ought to be placed where his imbecility could bring no dishonour upon the country hereafter.

Mr. C. would not now desert this expedition. He would force it to sea with all convenient despatch. He cared not who was sent out as a commander, if he was only qualified for the station.

He was willing that a midshipman, a lieutenant, or post-captain should be selected. He was disposed to leave this matter entirely to Executive discretion. He had only to say, that so far as his vote would effect it, the expedition should go to sea; he would not desert it; he would not thus reflect upon the acts of a former Congress. If the measure was proper two years ago, it was equally proper now. Not only were all the reasons for it as good now as they were at that time, but there were additional reasons. We had entered into the plan; we had made a beginning; we had gathered together the necessary materials; we had expended large sums of money, and we had raised great expectations. These would never all be realized; they had been considerably lowered by a series of unfortunate events, but the country had not yet lost all its interest in the measure. It was the character of the people to go ahead in every thing; and they expected to see this character developed by all their public servants. Whenever such servant failed in a great and important measure, or lagged in the performance of his duty, he very soon became the subject of animadversion and reprehension.

The gentleman from New-York, (Mr. Bronson,) had said that Congress, by voting the appropriation, authorized the employment of a frigate. Mr. C. voted for it, not because he approved of the frigate, but because he was unwilling to furnish an excuse, in the event of a failure, for charging that failure upon Congress. He wished the responsibility to rest on the commander of the expedition, who had insisted on having a frigate. That commander had had his own way; he had been indulged with just such a squadron as he asked for; and he had left it in the harbour of New-York, for the milder atmosphere of a more southern region. Mr. C. did not regret this determination. He had long since ceased to have any confidence in the success of the expedition as it was organized; and he was glad that an opportunity was afforded of placing it upon a proper footing. He believed that a similar feeling pervaded the whole country.

Washington Globe, 19*th April*, 1838.

As a mere matter of record to talent and character, the following inserted certificate will show, as evidence at an early date, the opinion of President Jefferson (unsolicited) relative to the ability of the author as a commander; but he being at the time bound by engagements to valuable friends in a command in the Pacific and China trade, whose support and means had enabled him already to have obtained the honour of important discoveries; his engagement, they being unwilling to grant his release, thus prevented him from moving, agreeably to his first wish, by accepting the honourable offer tendered, and thereby serving the remainder of his life in our gallant American navy.

CERTIFICATE.

New-York, January 19th, 1837.

This certifies that I was personally known to Mr. George Warner, on his return from Washington, having brought from President Jefferson an invitation and tender to Captain Edmund Fanning to the command of either of the new United States frigates, the New-York or Adams, as an inducement for him to enter into the naval service of government; his commission to take date the day the frigate was launched. This was, as my memory serves, between the years 1801 and 1803.

W. E. NEXSEN.

Attest, JOHN R. BLEECKER.

The annexed letters to the honourable Chairman of the Naval Committee of the House of Representatives of the American Congress assembled, will show the author's anxious regret at the unfortunate delay, and non-sailing of the South Sea National Exploring Expedition, in aiding the authorization of which by Congress he had acted so conspicuous a part. And herewith the public and general reader have the author's justification, which was so sacredly due to his profession and character, touching this exploring subject, after the part he had taken in procuring its authorization.

New-York, 21st April, 1838.

Dear Sir,

In the utmost respect and deference to all others, and their opinions, I cannot but now regret, extremely regret, that my experienced knowledge relating to such a Discovery and Exploring Expedition, in the construction of the proper vessels, its preparations and outfits, so early tendered to President Jackson, had not been accepted and used.

In the greatest respectful deference, I cannot but presume it would have enabled the expedition to have had the most efficient vessels, and been carried brilliantly into effect, to the great credit and benefit of the nation; as also nobly and shiningly to the American character, and that to an expense (I think) not exceeding half a million of dollars; but, alas! fate had not so decreed to the favour of our much beloved country,

I am, very respectfully,

Your obedient servant,

E. FANNING,

To the Hon. S. INGHAM, M. C.,
Chairman of the Naval Committee, H. R., United States' Congress, Washington city.

New-York, April 23d, 1838.

Dear Sir,

I have respectfully to observe that it has occurred to my mind, since mine of 21st inst., the propriety of an explanation, to prevent misconstruction, which I present herewith.

That after the great sacrifice of money and time made by me in the proceedings in aid to procure the authorization of a National Discovery and Exploring Expedition to the South Seas, &c., it does not appear that the omission of calling my experienced knowledge into requisition, in the construction of the most proper vessels, preparations in outfits, &c., was with our late venerable President, or the honourable Secretary of the Navy. Why? Because, in the correspondence between the latter and Commodore Jones, the Secretary, in his letter of date Navy Department, September 12th, 1836, has the following passage, viz.

"The person with whom you intimate I have corresponded, I presume, is Captain Edmund Fanning of New-York. Captain Fanning long since planned a South Sea Exploring Expedition, and has been urging it upon Congress ever since the administration of Mr. Madison. So far as there is a merit in suggesting and urging this measure, it is due to Captain Fanning. He is intimately acquainted with many regions which it is intended to explore; and it is very desirable to have the benefit of his knowledge and experience, both in fitting out and conducting the expedition."

Thus it will appear, that it was the desire of the President and Secretary that the humble aid of my practical knowledge in experience should be used to the enterprize, &c.

Having the honour to be,
Very respectfully,
Your obedient servant,
EDMUND FANNING.

Hon. S. Ingham, M. C., Chairman Naval Committee, H. R.
Washington city.

Thus, being not admitted to any part or voice in the preparations and outfits of the expedition, is not the author entirely clear as to its present unfavourable prospects, or its failure to the nation, should it end in such an unfortunate and unexpected result? This, it is hoped, the candid reader will frankly and generously admit, although the author took such an arduous and zealous part in aid of its authorization. At least, what is herein given will, in the opinion of the author, show what would be the most proper vessels for best effecting this exploring service, and why far preferable and better adapted than a ship of war.

In conclusion the author would remark, that the present unhappy situation of this important and popular national expedition again aroused the Yankee spirit of the old voyager, and called forth his voluntary patriotic aid, even at his time of life, once more to the help of his beloved country, in the support of this national measure. The following extract of a letter to His Excellency, the Vice-President of the United States, will show that the author has persevered to the end. But, alas! feeling, with the strong confidence of experience, that it cannot but be much feared that with ships of war,* all-important and beneficial discoveries will pass to the lot of other nations:—since who, acquainted with the affairs of the turf, would judge it wise for an active butcher to appear on the race-ground, mounted on a

* Except as a flag and home ship to the expedition.

large, fat, slick ox, with a view to take the purse from Eclipse, or his descendants, when the well-taught slayer of meats for the market, never having seen Eclipse run, depending on size and strength, had full confidence in his beautiful and noble animal?

Such is the difference between a heavy ship of war and the more proper and better adapted vessel, in navigating and exploring among the numerous ice islands, coral reefs, currents, &c. Hence the proposal in the extract of letter herein was given to furnish the most proper vessels, &c., for the performance of this new service to Americans. And with an earnest and zealous endeavour, with the most proper vessels as explorers, in room of ships of war, to carry this very favourite and laudable expedition through to a favourable termination, as well as to a most honourable and successful result.

EXTRACT.

New-York, May 19th, 1838.

Dear Sir,

I have respectfully to remark, that having, as you are aware, taken a zealous part, to the sacrifice of much time and expense, in the aid to the procuring an act, authorizing a National South Sea Exploring Expedition, relating to which, unfortunately, in its preparation and fit out, there has arisen at a great expenditure, serious disappointment and difficulty, which, in all respectful deference, I cannot but presume to think, that, if my experienced knowledge, that was so early tendered in good faith previous to any appointment, or the subject being taken up for action, by a note, through your kindness, to our then venerable President, had been acccepted and used, it would have tended to have brought about a quite different result, than the expedition's present situation. I, therefore, after the part I have voluntarily acted to its authorization, have come to the resolution to again respectfully tender all within my humble means, and in all respectful deference to propose to Government the following suggestion and expedient. * * * * *

I know not if, by the clause providing the vessels in the

authorization act, whether this proposal in tender be admissible:—but if it so be, then, in the view of a trial to aid in the support of the American character, and to endeavour to accomplish and carry into effect a similar favourite national enterprise, this suggested proposal is hereby tendered in the purest zeal, and spirit of real patriotism—in aid to the measure—feeling confident, with only this proposed governmental aid, with the means at the author's control, that there can be fitted out an efficient squadron to excel in performing a Discovery and Exploring Enterprise to those seas. This can, with the right vessels, be organized with the primest force our country affords for such service, as a number of the most experienced, able, and talented nautical citizens in the Merchant Marine will readily volunteer in such an expedition.

I am confident this will show to the world, that American seamen, when they engage on a task, if ever so arduous, know how to accomplish it, to bring honour to the American character, as well as great benefit to the nation. Therefore, if the herein suggested proposal and project be approved and accepted by Government, I herewith pledge all my means, with best exertions, and all that is dear to a citizen, to faithfully use every endeavour to carry the enterprise (the danger of the seas and extraordinary occurrences excepted,) with all despatch through, in its intended performance, and to the best possible effect, by calling to its aid and into requisition, every promising ability, exertion, perseverance, &c., that can tend to bring honour, credit, and benefit to the nation.

With high regard,

I am, dear sir, very respectfully,

Your obdt. servt.

EDMUND FANNING.

To His Excellency

RICHARD M. JOHNSON,

Vice-President of the United States,

Washington City.

The suggested and tendered proposal was, after mature consideration of the clause in the authorization act, considered not admissible. May 28th, 1838.

The author would here respectfully add, in explanation to what is contained in this volume, viz:—The remark, that if he had never existed, or been among the living, the authorization of this National Exploring Expedition would not, at its time of passage, have been by Congress authorized:—that by this, he is far from meaning to convey the idea that he should ever have obtained it, if the zealous co-operation and aid of other worthy citizens had not been given. But that it was by his, and the united perseverance of those other patriotic citizens, that its sanction by Congress was procured. The author, *as related*, broke the ice, as it were, and cleared away the prior difficulty. And if this had not firstly been done, the sanction of an Explorer's law could not have been obtained.

NOTE.—The American Exploring Expedition consists, as now (June, 1838,) organized, under the command of Lieutenant Commandant Wilkes, as follows, viz.—

Vessels.			*Men.*
Vincennes,	Sloop of war,	- - - -	120
Peacock,	Do.	do. - - - -	105
Porpoise,	Brig	do. - - - -	50
Relief,	Store Ship,	- - - - -	70

INDEX

THE END

ATTACK AND MASSACRE OF CREW OF

HIS IS BELIEVED TO BE THE ONLY KNOW